# STATE
*of the*
# STRUGGLE

## REPORT ON THE BATTLE
## AGAINST GLOBAL TERRORISM

Lee Hamilton, Bruce Hoffman
Brian Jenkins, Paul Pillar, Xavier Raufer
Walter Reich, Fernando Reinares

*edited by*
Justine A. Rosenthal

COUNCIL ON GLOBAL TERRORISM
*Washington, D.C.*

Original release date September 6, 2006

*State of the Struggle: Report on the Battle against Global Terrorism*
may be ordered from:
BROOKINGS INSTITUTION PRESS
c/o HFS, P.O. Box 50370, Baltimore, MD 21211-4370
Tel.: 800/537-5487, 410/516-6956; Fax: 410/516-6998; Internet: www.brookings.edu

*Library of Congress Cataloging-in-Publication Data*

State of the struggle : report on the battle against global terrorism / Lee Hamilton . . .
[et al.] ; edited by Justine A. Rosenthal.
p.   cm.
Summary: "Assesses the West's progress across a wide array of counterterrorism
imperatives. From ethical questions of balancing security and core values to the problems
of creating viable counterterrorism coalitions to the likelihood of biological, chemical,
and nuclear weapons, report examines a wide swath of issues necessary to create
workable counterterrorism strategies"—Provided by publisher.
Includes bibliographical references and index.
ISBN-13: 978-0-8157-3411-6 (pbk. : alk. paper)
ISBN-10: 0-8157-3411-5 (pbk. : alk. paper)
1. Terrorism. 2. Terrorism—Prevention. 3. Terrorism—United States—Prevention.
I. Hamilton, Lee. II. Rosenthal, Justine A. III. Council on Global Terrorism.
HV6431.S723 2007
363.325—dc22                                    2006103295

1 2 3 4 5 6 7 8 9

The paper used in this publication meets minimum requirements of the
American National Standard for Information Sciences—Permanence
of Paper for Printed Library Materials: ANSI Z39.48-1992.

Cover photo © Corbis. All rights reserved.
Cover design by Chris Donovan

Typeset in Sabon and Optima

Composition by Cynthia Stock
Silver Spring, Maryland

Printed by Victor Graphics
Baltimore, Maryland

# Contents

# Acknowledgments

This report stems from discussions and interviews of the founding members of the Council on Global Terrorism. The hope was to create an easily accessible but detailed assessment of the current state of the struggle against global extremism. If we managed to achieve our goals, it was largely due to the help of others.

None of this work would have been possible without David Bradley. His spirit of generosity and ability to herd cats only skim the surface of his contribution. He is the very genesis of this project and provided a forum for us to share our thoughts, all the while enforcing a much needed organizational structure—often against our mighty protestations—undoubtedly making for a far better book. We are in his debt.

The group is also grateful to James Kitfield. His ability to weave together our thoughts, the facts of the case, and a narrative, created a far more cohesive product than we could have managed without him. His probing questions, background study, and masterful storytelling, provided the voice for this project.

Many thanks to Alex Christine Douglas as well, for her research, fact-checking and administrative help, all vital to making the product a reality. As with any endeavor of this sort, the book is immeasurably better for their contributions. Any missteps remain the authors' domain.

## SENSE OF THE CONVERSATION, NOT MORE

It is important to make less, not more, occasion about the issuance of this preliminary report, first released in September 2006. It represents what we believe to be very intelligent, very grounded, worrisomely-sober, views about the state of the global struggle against terrorism. But, there is nothing official about the publication. This work was commissioned by no official body. It is released to no expectant audience. It is simpler, maybe more honest, by dint of the fact that its writing represents the uninflected views of experts in wholly private conversation.

Across the course of several months, this small, informal group of experts on global terrorism met several times to exchange views. Individually, they met with interviewers to expand on their comments. Privately, they filled out a report card on their sense of how the parts of the terrorism struggle are faring. (Largely, not well.)

The resulting report aggregates the group and individual conversations. What results is, as in a Quaker meeting, the larger sense of the group, nothing more. There is no requirement or achievement of unanimity; as to some points, the experts disagree. The best that can be said is that on the larger issues there is broad —if not uniform—agreement. It is this larger sense, not unanimous view, that this report is intended to convey.

# Combating Islamic Extremist Terrorism

OVERALL
GRADE D+

| | |
|---|---|
| Al-Qaeda headquarters | C+ |
| Al-Qaeda affiliated groups | C– |
| Al-Qaeda seeded groups | D+ |
| Al-Qaeda inspired groups | D |
| Sympathizers | D– |

Five years after the September 11 attacks, is the United States winning or losing the global "war on terror"? Depending on the prism through which one views the conflict or the metrics used to gauge success, the answers to the question are starkly different.

The fact that the American homeland has not suffered another attack since 9/11 certainly amounts to a major achievement. U.S. military and security forces have dealt al-Qaeda a severe blow, capturing or killing roughly three-quarters of its pre-9/11 leadership and denying the terrorist group uncontested sanctuary in Afghanistan. The United States and its allies have also thwarted numerous terrorist plots around the world—most recently a plan by British Muslims to simultaneously blow up as many as ten jetliners bound for major American cities.

Now adjust the prism. To date, al-Qaeda's top leaders have survived the superpower's most punishing blows, adding to the near-mythical status they enjoy among Islamic extremists. The terrorism they inspire has continued apace in a deadly cadence of attacks, from Bali and Istanbul to Madrid, London, and Mumbai. Even discounting the violence in Iraq and Afghanistan, the tempo of terrorist attacks—the coin of the realm in the jihadi enterprise—is actually greater today than before 9/11.

Meanwhile, U.S. military forces continue to strain under the burden of a bloody and unpopular war in Iraq. Scandals at Abu Ghraib and Guantánamo Bay have handed extremist Islamic ideologues a propaganda bonanza, and there is every sign that radicalization in the Muslim world is spreading rather than shrinking.

"The United States has always looked at this conflict with Islamic extremists from a Western perspective and assumed we were winning the war on terror, but if you look at it through the enemy's eyes you may get a different answer," said Bruce Hoffman, professor at Georgetown University's Edmund A. Walsh School of Foreign Service and a member of the Council on Global Terrorism. Al-Qaeda's metric of success, he contends, is not determined by the lifespan of a presidential administration or by a midterm election cycle. "Rather, they are fighting a long war of attrition in hopes of draining our resolve and lulling us into a pre-9/11 sense of complacency. Already they see our military becoming bogged down and bled dry in Iraq and Afghanistan; our economy is straining under the weight of multiple wars and rising energy costs; and the American public's confidence in the Bush administration's conduct of the war in Iraq has steadily eroded and could eventually impact public support for the war on terrorism. Most importantly, al-Qaeda has survived our strongest blows, which has given an enormous boost to their belief in the historical inevitability and righteousness of their cause."

So, is the United States really winning or losing the global war on terrorism? In many ways the question itself reflects the great complexities and challenges of this conflict. In actuality, the United States is not engaged in a war on terrorism. Terrorism is a tactic of the weak against the strong. The enemy we confront has a specific nature, and to cast it as global "terror" risks missing its multifaceted dimensions and true character.

"The mere fact that five years after 9/11 we are still struggling to define the enemy and understand why it hates us is indicative of the vast challenge we face, because if you can't define your enemy with precision, it's very hard to develop an effective counterterrorism strategy," said Lee Hamilton, president of the Woodrow Wilson International Center for Scholars and a member of the Council on Global Terrorism. Casting this as a "global war on terror," he added, has also led to an emphasis on military action in a way that unhelpfully overshadows other aspects of the struggle.

"The military undoubtedly has an important role to play, but an effective counterterrorism strategy will have to do a much better job of integrating all tools of American power, including public and international diplomacy, law enforcement, money tracking, intelligence, homeland security, and foreign aid," said Hamilton, former vice chair of the 9/11 commission. "Military action and the attendant violence and killing garners all the headlines, but we really have to better coordinate all of those functions into a synergistic counterterrorism policy."

Describing the conflict as a global "war on terror" has the added disadvantage of suggesting that it is easily bound in time, with a distinct beginning, middle, and end. That plays to American impatience and fosters a military strategy of decapitation and attrition of the enemy. In truth, the conflict more closely resembles a global insurgency, and successful counterinsurgency campaigns are protracted, always emphasizing the ideological battle for minds at least as much as military action.

In the wake of the 9/11 attacks, there was an understandable focus on Osama bin Laden and his top lieutenants, as well as the substantial infrastructure that al-Qaeda had established in Afghanistan. Yet in the interceding years, it became clear that al-Qaeda was at the core of an interlinked "network of networks," and never quite as hierarchical or monolithic an organization as was routinely depicted in and by the media.

Since 9/11, Islamic extremist terrorism has morphed into a multidimensional network with five primary nodes:

— al-Qaeda headquarters and its global infrastructure of cells and individual operatives;

— al-Qaeda-affiliated terrorist groups with loose linkages to al-Qaeda, such as Jemaah Islamiyah (JI) in Indonesia, the Islamic Movement of Uzbekistan (IMU), the Moro Islamic Liberation Front (MILF) in the Philippines, and Lashkar-e-Taiba (LeT) in Kashmir, all of which have received spiritual or operational guidance and assistance from bin Laden;

— al-Qaeda-seeded groups, like those responsible for the London and Madrid transit system bombings, comprising one or two members with some al-Qaeda-headquarters contact, whether it be training, participating in a prior jihadi campaign, or operational planning;

— homegrown "self-starter" cells of Islamic extremists with no clear connection to al-Qaeda but incited by bin Laden's radical ideology; and

— the pool of Muslims who are sympathetic to the goals and ideas of radical Islam, even if sometimes disapproving of bin Laden's terrorist methods.

The linkages between these organisms and the relative vitality and health of each is constantly shifting and evolving depending on the environment. Over time, counterterrorism antidotes that threaten one organism can cause the others to mutate and evolve; one tentacle may be made weaker, only strengthening another.

"Because we are so mechanically oriented in the West, we tend to think of organizations as shaped hierarchically like a pyramid, with the leaders at the top and the workers at the bottom, and everyone a cog in the machine," said Xavier Raufer, director of studies and research in the Research Department on the Contemporary Criminal Menace at the Paris Institute of Criminology, University of Paris II, and a member of the Council on Global Terrorism. "Al-Qaeda was always based more on a biological model, which is messier and more ill-defined, but also very resilient. Think of the global Islamic jihadist movement like water that ebbs and flows and occasionally coagulates and freezes into ice in places such as Sudan and Afghanistan, only to melt again under pressure. In that ecosystem of radical Islam, Osama bin Laden's preachings pour forth like rain, and mushrooms sprout in Jakarta, Madrid, and London."

## Al-Qaeda Headquarters

There is no doubt that the U.S. campaign targeting al-Qaeda's headquarters and its Taliban benefactors has significantly damaged the group's operations. Top leaders Osama bin Laden and Ayman al-Zawahiri are in hiding, the group's pre-9/11 leadership is largely destroyed, and 9/11 mastermind Khalid Shaikh Mohammed has been captured. Al-Qaeda has also lost the infrastructure and sanctuary in Afghanistan that allowed it to methodically plan operations. Though it continues to function, its ability to scout and train thousands of Islamic extremists over a period of years is greatly weakened.

Brian Jenkins, a longtime counterterrorism expert, senior advisor to the president of the RAND Corporation, and a member of the Council on Global Terrorism, pointed out: "Denying 'al-Qaeda Central' its former sanctuary in Afghanistan was critical to degrading its operational capabilities. Al-Qaeda used those training camps in Afghanistan almost like an NBA combine. They attracted potential recruits from all over the globe, and through a training regimen identified the most talented or capable people in terms of their skills or dedication. The loss of that sanctuary has thus made life considerably tougher for al-Qaeda."

Yet, al-Qaeda has long demonstrated unusual resiliency. The organization used the decade of the 1990s to establish deep roots, allowing it to weather the United States' counterterrorism campaign. The rapid replacement of leaders captured or killed in that effort also suggests that al-Qaeda had a deeper "bench" of relatively experienced operatives than many experts initially anticipated. Bin Laden, al-Zawahiri, and other top operatives, intelligence services now believe, have found sanctuary, if not altogether safe haven, in the tribal regions on the Pakistan side of the border with Afghanistan, an area that lies outside the effective control of the central government in Islamabad.

"In terms of terrorist sanctuaries and potential sanctuaries, there's a natural tendency to avert our eyes and shift our concerns away from these ungoverned spaces because they are often too difficult or horrible to contemplate, but we will quickly pay the price for such neglect," said Walter Reich, Yitzhak Rabin Memorial Professor of International Affairs, Ethics and Human Behavior at George Washington University and a member of the Council of Global Terrorism. "The lesson of Afghanistan was that any ungoverned area that is within the reach of Islamic extremists is a danger and matter of great concern."

In terms of al-Qaeda cells and key international operatives, however, the lack of a successful attack on the U.S. homeland since 9/11 at least strongly suggests that the group had little infrastructure established inside the United States prior to or after the attacks. In contrast, European counterterrorism experts noted evidence of strong linkages between al-Qaeda headquarters and terrorist cells that conducted both the Madrid and London transit bombings in 2004 and 2005, respectively. In the case of the Madrid bombings, the attackers were essentially remnants of an al-Qaeda cell in Spain broken up in the winter of 2001; in the case of the London bombings, ringleader Mohammed Siddique Khan is believed to have trained in an al-Qaeda camp, returning to Pakistan before the bombing. Al-Qaeda's media arm later released Khan's martyrdom video. On the first anniversary of the London bombings, one of Khan's accomplices, Shahzad Tanweer, was also memorialized on tape. Both videos contained commentary from al-Zawahiri, adding evidence of ties between these attacks and al-Qaeda. More recently, the group of Islamic extremists in Britain who plotted to blow up jetliners flying to the United States also had ties to Pakistan and suspected al-Qaeda operatives.

"There is no doubt that al-Qaeda has been much weakened in terms of its ability to communicate and coordinate operations as a result of losing sanctuary in Afghanistan, but in Europe we have seen a lot of evidence that al-Qaeda operatives are still actively planning multiple major attacks and hoping to perpetrate another 9/11-type spectacular," said Fernando Reinares, director of the Programme on Global Terrorism at Spain's Elcano Royal Institute for International and Strategic Studies, professor of political science and security studies at Rey Juan Carlos University, and a member of the Council on Global Terrorism. "As it adapts to an increasingly hostile environment, al-Qaeda is becoming far more decentralized and reliant on affiliated groups and individuals, and bin Laden has focused on articulating jihadi ideology. I reject the idea, however, that it has now evolved completely into a movement or ideology. Al-Qaeda is still an organization with operatives planning attacks, and I fear the next successful al-Qaeda spectacular will most likely occur in Europe."

## Al-Qaeda Affiliates

From an early stage, one attribute that made Osama bin Laden particularly dangerous was his skill in coalescing several groups under his pan-Islamic banner. A mosaic of Islamic extremist groups have been drawn to bin Laden's messianic message of war between Western and

Islamic civilizations, and his calls for jihad or "holy war" against America and its allies. Al-Qaeda became so lethal in such a short period of time in part because it established itself as the leading part of a coalition of as many as twenty Islamist terrorist organizations stretching around the world. Indeed, it was the watershed merger with the Egyptian Islamic Jihad in 1998 that brought al-Qaeda the considerable organizational skills of Ayman al-Zawahiri and elevated the jihadi struggle from a more myopic battle—against first the Russians and then Saudi Arabia—to the larger struggle against the "near enemy" in the Middle East and the "far enemy" in the West.

Since 9/11, these al-Qaeda-affiliated groups, or Islamic extremist groups that embrace al-Qaeda's agenda, have been responsible for much of the terrorist carnage around the world. Most recently, the Kashmiri separatist group Lashkar-e-Taiba allegedly had a hand in the train bombings in Mumbai, India, this past July that killed 197 passengers. That group is inspired by the same Saudi-style Wahhabism as bin Laden, and hopes to bring the Indian subcontinent under Muslim rule; the pace of its attacks continues to ratchet upward. In similar fashion, Salafia Jihadia, a group with close ties to al-Qaeda, carried out the Casablanca bombings of May 2003. A series of attacks on Western interests and oil infrastructure in Saudi Arabia in 2004 were conducted by al-Qaeda in Saudi Arabia, and much of the ongoing sectarian violence in Iraq was provoked by al-Qaeda in Iraq. Four bombings in Bali and Jakarta, Indonesia; Taba, Egypt; and General Santos City, the Philippines, were the work of Jemaah Islamiyah, yet another Islamist terrorist group with close ties to al-Qaeda. The list goes on.

The United States and its allies continue to wage pitched battles with these terrorist groups, often with mixed results. U.S. forces in Iraq scored a major victory earlier this year when they killed the terrorist Abu Musab al-Zarqawi, the extremely violent leader of al-Qaeda in Iraq. Yet the sectarian violence that al-Zarqawi dreamed of stoking into an all-out civil war continues unabated. Significantly, al-Zarqawi's chosen successor is a former member of the Egyptian Islamic Jihad with close ties to Ayman al-Zawahiri—an indicator that al-Qaeda is bringing the Iraq conflict further under its direct control.

"Despite a concerted effort by the terrorists to give al-Qaeda in Iraq an Iraqi face, the fact that an Egyptian and former protégé of Zawahiri was chosen to lead the group shows that al-Qaeda continues to exert significant influence on these affiliated groups," said Bruce Hoffman.

Much like al-Qaeda itself, a number of affiliated Islamic extremist groups have also shown an ability to continue terrorist attacks and planning even after the death or capture of key leaders. Despite the arrest or incapacitation of many of Jemaah Islamiyah's top operatives, for instance, the group still remains a deadly threat, continuing to plot and terrorize, all the while training new members, expanding its reach, and bringing other groups like those in the Philippines into its fold.

That ability to decentralize operations and replenish ranks despite top personnel losses helps explain the resiliency of the terrorism network of networks. In one such example, Indonesian authorities recently raided a Jemaah Islamiyah safe house, killing two top lieutenants and nearly capturing leader Noordin Mohammed Top. Inside the house, police officials found bombs already assembled and plans for additional attacks. Yet the documents seized by authorities revealed just how meticulous the JI leaders were in passing along their bomb-making and other terrorism skills to the next cadre of operatives.

## Homegrown Terrorism

Last November, Australian authorities also raided two so-called self-starter cells of Islamic extremists in Sydney and Melbourne composed almost entirely of second-generation immigrants and Australian citizens with no apparent connection to al-Qaeda, other than an embrace of bin Laden's radical ideology. This is part of a phenomenon of homegrown terrorism: In some cases, like in Madrid and London, adherents are directed by more established al-Qaeda operatives; in others, the phenomenon is represented by purely independent acts of violence, like the murder of filmmaker Theo van Gogh in the Netherlands. The recent roll up of cells of Islamic extremists in Britain, Canada, and the United States represents one of the most worrisome trends in Islamic extremist terrorism. Authorities need to better understand what forces in the broader community of Muslims are conspiring to persuade people with only a normal interest in religion to suddenly become radicalized.

Paul Pillar, visiting professor at Georgetown University's Center for Peace and Security Studies, former national intelligence officer for the Near East and South Asia, and a member of the Council on Global Terrorism, said: "The U.S.-led offensive against al-Qaeda has scored significant successes against the group's upper and mid-level tiers, but the organization has mutated, and the radical jihadist threat has become more decentralized and diffuse. That evolution worries me because we now have more potential threats, which are difficult to track from an intelligence point of view, coming at us from lots of different directions. And of all those threats, the homegrown cells really keep me awake at night. Often we don't even know they exist. Yet if just a handful of these guys had hijacked one airplane and flown it into one of the World Trade Center towers on 9/11, they still would have killed 1,500 people."

The idea that terrorist groups can come together virtually spontaneously and wreak major havoc with minimal funding or training shows how pernicious this evolving threat will become with little or no way to tell who will become radicalized. Its growing occurrence, and an increase in potential recruits and sympathizers, creates a new level of threat. This phenomenon is crucial to how great a danger we face, for how long, and in which regions of the world. This fifth node of al-Qaeda—the groundswell of sympathizers—is key to the future of this battle; its unique characteristics are addressed in fuller detail in chapter 7.

Next, the Council on Global Terrorism will examine steps the United States and its allies have taken to hone their counterterrorism capabilities. ■

# Improving U.S. and Coalition Counterterrorism Capabilities

# 2

| | OVERALL GRADE | C |
|---|---|---|
| Reforming intelligence capabilities | | C |
| Improving law enforcement capabilities | | C– |
| Transforming military capabilities | | C |
| Improving money tracking capabilities | | C+ |
| Cooperation & coordination between branches of government | | C– |
| Cooperation & coordination between local, state, and federal government | | D+ |
| Cooperation & coordination between allies | | B– |

The enemy that struck the United States with a surprise assault on September 11, 2001, was well-known. As soon as counterterrorism experts witnessed a second airplane flying into one of the World Trade Center towers in New York, most suspected the nation was under attack by the al-Qaeda terrorist organization led by Osama bin Laden. Yet despite all that was understood about the enemy and all that foreshadowed a pending attack on the American homeland, the essential details of the 9/11 plot eluded U.S. intelligence services. The movements and activities of the terrorists likewise largely escaped the notice of law-enforcement agencies. That failure points to the central role that better intelligence and law-enforcement investigation must play in illuminating the shadowy world inhabited by terrorists, in order to expose such people before their plots reach a terrible conclusion.

An awareness of these necessities propelled the U.S. government to implement the most far-reaching reforms of its vast intelligence apparatus in half a century. A director-of-national-intelligence position was created and given the authority to coordinate the activities and cross talk between stovepiped intelligence services. A new National Counterterrorism Center (NCTC) that reports to the director of national intelligence (DNI) was established to focus on terrorism and fuse information collected by disparate agencies on both domestic and foreign threats. The center now analyzes information from twenty-six separate databases, sharing its insights with an estimated 5,500 users throughout the federal government.

For its part, the CIA has refocused its efforts on the critical task of human intelligence collection, reportedly initiating a major increase in the number of its operations officers stationed overseas. The Pentagon created the post of undersecretary of defense for intelligence, and greatly expanded the capabilities of the U.S. Special Operations Command in the realm of counterterrorism intelligence gathering and manhunting. The successful tracking and killing of al-Zarqawi in Iraq by elite units combining U.S. Special Operations Forces and intelligence operatives from the CIA and Defense Intelligence Agency was also a signature achievement, and it showed how increased cooperation between services can be vital to on-the-ground success. Domestically, the FBI elevated counterterrorism to its number one priority, establishing sixty-five new joint terrorism task forces around the country that are staffed by FBI agents and state and local law-enforcement officers. The FBI also runs the Terrorist Screening Center (responsible for consolidating the various terrorist watch lists compiled by federal agencies) and has begun coordinating with the Department of Homeland Security in communicating terrorism-related intelligence bulletins to local law-enforcement agencies. Meanwhile, the Department of Homeland Security has its own intelligence shop, the Information Analysis Unit, and the Treasury Department has established a special bureau devoted to tracking and blocking terrorist financing.

"After 9/11, it was wise for the U.S. government to do everything possible to sharpen its intelligence-gathering tools, because good intelligence will be a major part of the solution to Islamic extremist terrorism," said Lee Hamilton. "On the other hand, it's important to recognize that there are real limitations on just how good our intelligence can be. Essentially, trying to penetrate a terrorist cell is the toughest challenge in the world of intelligence gathering."

There is still ample evidence that the effort to coordinate cross talk between myriad federal agencies, and to fuse counterterrorism intelligence into a coherent picture, is far from complete. According to a report by Congress's Government Accountability Office earlier this year, the Bush administration has yet to comprehensively improve counterterrorism intelligence sharing between federal agencies, and between those agencies and thousands of state and local law-enforcement departments; this despite nearly five years of legislation, presidential directives, and executive orders designed to do just that.

"There has been marked improvement, extending back well before 9/11, in the coordination between the FBI and CIA, but there's plenty of room for more improvement in terms of overall counterterrorism intelligence sharing and fusion," said Paul Pillar.

"After the next successful terrorist attack, I'm sure we'll see another multimillion-dollar commission whose investigation shows disconnects among federal intelligence agencies, or between those agencies and local law enforcement. To a certain degree, that's the inevitable nature of large bureaucracies."

## Multinational Intelligence Sharing

Despite the inevitable setbacks involved in such a massive reorganization, the United States can claim some successes as a result of the priority given to improving its own capabilities, as well as working more effectively with other governments to better track terrorists. Not only have the United States government and its partners captured or killed roughly three-quarters of al-Qaeda's pre-9/11 leadership; many of those arrests were made in Pakistan in conjunction with Pakistani intelligence services.

The recent arrests by British authorities of more than a score of British Muslims of Pakistani ancestry who were hatching an ambitious plot to blow up transatlantic jetliners (and subsequent arrests in Pakistan itself) also point to real and useful intelligence sharing between nations. President Bush has spoken publicly of thwarting at least ten other major terrorist attacks since September 2001, and, in the past year, suspected Islamic extremist terrorist cells were rolled up in places as disparate as Australia, Canada, Lebanon, and the United States. As important, intelligence and law-enforcement agencies have thus far succeeded in thwarting further attacks on the U.S. homeland.

"Britain's foiling of the recent terrorist plot involving transatlantic air traffic, and arrests in Pakistan that suggest an al-Qaeda connection, underscore once again how utterly dependent we are on close intelligence cooperation with our allies," said Bruce Hoffman. The fact that the suspected terrorists found it necessary to attack the United States from the outside also suggests, he said, that the single biggest accomplishment of the U.S. government's entire counterterrorism campaign has been the denial to al-Qaeda of any apparent infrastructure inside the United States. "That means that al-Qaeda will have to continue to try and strike us from the outside, or else import terrorists into this country, and that's a riskier proposition that presents intelligence and law-enforcement agencies with more opportunities to expose terrorist cells. Despite those successes, however, this latest plot indicates that al-Qaeda remains an adaptive enemy that is still trying to strike us with acts of 'superterrorism.'"

When an Italian prosecutor accused Italian intelligence agents of conspiring with their U.S. counterparts in the capture and secret extradition of a suspected Islamic terrorist in Italy, he pointed a rare spotlight on the unusually close cooperative arrangements that have developed between allied intelligence agencies as a direct outgrowth of 9/11 and subsequent attacks. Essentially, few nations now feel immune to the threat, and in ways both seen and unseen, they are increasingly finding common cause against Islamic extremist terrorism.

"Rising international concerns about terrorism have led to improved intelligence sharing and even dialogue between the United States and some pretty strange bedfellows such as Libya," said Paul Pillar. "Muammar Qaddafi went from practicing and supporting terrorism in the 1970s and 1980s to cooperating on counterterrorism out of his own fear of the radical Islamists. So, while most intelligence cooperation is still conducted on a bilateral basis given concerns about the leaking of classified information, it is probably better today than ever. We're also seeing that counterterrorism cooperation often remains strong even when nations have other political disagreements."

The investigation into the 2002 Bali bombings serves as another prime example of this intelligence-cooperation dynamic. That attack and subsequent incidents aimed at Western targets were perpetrated by Jemaah Islamiyah. After the initial Bali bombings, which killed 202 people, including 88 Australians, Australia sent intelligence, police, and forensic experts to Indonesia to assist with the investigation, and the team has remained in place ever since. Even when the overall relationship between Indonesia and Australia hit a rough patch over the issue of immigration—and Indonesia withdrew its ambassador to Australia—the close counterterrorism cooperation continued. Largely as a result, the joint Indonesian-Australian investigation has led to the capture or death of more than 200 members of Jemaah Islamiyah.

Cooperation among European countries and one-on-one intelligence sharing between the United States and countries like Spain, France, and Germany are particularly strong.

"In the intelligence business, bilateral cooperation works very well, and European countries have experienced particularly viable cooperation nation-state to nation-state," said Xavier Raufer. "When it is multilateral and third parties are involved, you might compromise a source or an informer, the information may get sold, and it is harder to trace leaks. Multilateral intelligence cooperation simply doesn't work. We need to understand what cooperation is useful, and what less so, in this tricky world of intelligence. And so far, the Europeans have seen real success."

The United States can boast similar accomplishments in working with Western counterparts. "The cooperation between European countries and the U.S., in general terms, is excellent," said Fernando Reinares. "The exchanges are secure, trustworthy, and effective. There has been an increase in the amount and quality of the police and intelligence cooperation."

Of course, the groundwork for all of this counterterrorism intelligence sharing and cooperation is nothing new—it was laid over a period of decades. Like-minded nations realized long ago that Islamic extremist terrorism was a growing threat, and their intelligence and law-enforcement agencies began forming ties in order to better combat it. September 11 and subsequent attacks by Islamic extremist terrorists simply solidified and strengthened those ties.

"The intelligence-sharing structure and counterterrorism coalition we see today has actually been twenty-five years or more in the making," said Brian Jenkins. "What the 9/11 attacks did was create an unprecedented focus and collective sense of urgency for our counterterrorism efforts. And it is interesting that that unanimity of purpose and cooperation on intelligence matters has continued despite very sharp political differences on issues such as Iraq."

Even still, inevitable weaknesses remain. Osama bin Laden's success in evading capture and al-Qaeda's continued hatching of terrorist plots also point to the organization's ability to adapt to U.S. and coalition intelligence operations. Despite being on the run and in hiding since 9/11, bin Laden has managed to maintain a steady stream of communications through audio- and videotapes smuggled to Arabic-language radio and television stations. Terrorists have increasingly exploited the relative anonymity of the Internet to communicate, indoctrinate, and recruit.

The relative lack of expertise in Arabic language and culture also remains a weakness that Islamic extremist terrorists have successfully exploited. "Osama bin Laden and Ayman al-Zawahiri are still at large because they have an Arabic frame of mind and cultural background that is absolutely lost in translation in terms of our intelligence gathering," said Xavier Raufer. "Terrorist watch lists assembled in the West are often obsolete as soon as the ink is dry, for instance, because there might be many thousands of men at any one time with the name 'Ali Mohammed Baghdadi.'"

In the megacities of the developing world such as Karachi, São Paulo, or Lagos, said Raufer, electronic spying is also of limited effectiveness because the terrorists commonly use stolen cell phones and speak in culturally encrypted code. "Even the vast efforts to spy on e-mail transmissions around the world failed to pick up on the 9/11 plot. The terrorists simply maneuvered around it—sending letters and staying off computers. I really worry that this Western reliance on high-tech intelligence gathering—over human intelligence and cultural understanding—represents the equivalent of the French Maginot Line in this conflict."

## Tracking Terrorist Financing

Even with that understanding, efforts to lay bare the underground plots of the terrorists must continue on multiple fronts. As recent news reports about the Terrorist Finance Tracking Program reveal, a major avenue paved in the U.S.-led counterterrorism campaign is the

Treasury Department's move to track and block terrorist financing. The hope is that by cutting terrorist funding streams, one not only limits the tactical scope and capabilities of terrorist organizations but also creates a valuable intelligence tool to illuminate terrorist networks and their clandestine financiers.

"The original idea behind tracking and blocking terrorist funding was to starve the beast, and the Treasury Department did develop some very sophisticated tools to identify terrorist funding streams— so much so that they came to see the intelligence gathered in the process as the greatest value," said Lee Hamilton, co-author of *Without Precedent: The Inside Story of the 9/11 Commission.* "Unfortunately, the terrorists adapted very quickly by turning to more informal ways of transferring money. As a result, despite all of our sophistication, we have neither starved the beast nor produced very good intelligence on how exactly these organizations continue to finance themselves. They tend to operate below our radar screens in that regard."

Certainly attempts to block funding streams in an effort to keep pressure on groups continue to make sense. While it is probably impossible to deter an Islamic extremist who is willing to die in a suicide attack, it may be quite possible to deter wealthy and prominent individuals or established charities by exposing their ties to terrorism. And large terrorist organizations do require significant financing to recruit operatives, take care of their members' families, run training camps, plan operations, and bribe officials. In the 1990s, for example, al-Qaeda's financial support largely kept the Egyptian Islamic Jihad in operation, eventually leading to a de facto merger of the two terrorist groups. Recently, the diversion of earthquake-relief funds by a Pakistani charity reportedly helped tip British authorities to the jetliner plot—a sign that these efforts are not without their rewards.

In the final analysis, however, individual attacks are cheap enough to mount—and money flows freely enough to terrorist groups through informal channels—that it would be unwise to put too much confidence in our ability to thwart terrorism by bankrupting the infrastructure. The devastating 2005 suicide attacks on the London transit system only cost an estimated $15,000 to stage. Terrorist groups in the Middle East and South Asia also have proven adept at exploiting informal hawala money-exchange systems in which actual cash need never change hands. Instead, someone merely signs a slip of paper in Karachi and the money appears in Dubai, or vice versa. Council members also draw little confidence from intercepted communications between terrorists who complain about a lack of funds.

"We're always seeing intercepted letters or communications from terrorists who are griping about not having enough money, but that's just human nature," said Walter Reich. "Everyone wants more money and complains about not having enough, and the terrorists are no different. To read into those comments the implication that terrorists can no longer afford to mount attacks would be a mistake."

The very nature of terrorism as a tool of the weak against the strong puts significant limits on the effectiveness of interdicting funds. Though these programs yield intelligence and may deter more "traditional" donors—both worthy accomplishments—on another level, terrorists simply dive deeper into the murky waters of the illicit global economy to cobble together the limited money needed to launch attacks. Significant amounts of money from Afghanistan's vast trade in opium, for instance, are thought to be siphoned off by the Taliban and al-Qaeda.

At the end of the day, no matter how good our intelligence, no matter the efficacy of our programs, no matter the level of cooperation, even 99 percent success means more attacks in the United States, against allies, and around the world. "Given that terrorist organizations are ruthless in dealing with anyone suspected of being an informant, and that terrorist cells involve small numbers of people highly conscious of operational security, it always has been and always will be extremely difficult to penetrate terrorist cells," said Paul Pillar. "Yet penetrating them is often the only way to get information specific enough to foil an attack. So while we have to continue making every effort to penetrate them, we also have to recognize that there will always be some plots that we miss." ∎

# Creating an Effective Coalition to Fight Terrorism

3

| | OVERALL GRADE | C– |
|---|---|---|
| Creating effective, regional counterterrorism coalitions | | C |
| Enlisting great powers in the counterterrorism effort | | C+ |
| Bringing Muslim nations into the war on terror | | C– |
| European Union-U.S. cooperation in the war on terror | | B– |
| Passage of effective laws to strengthen international counterterrorism standards | | C– |
| Efforts to help willing but weak states better police territory and deny terrorist groups safe havens | | C– |
| Deterring state sponsorship of terrorism | | C– |

In the wake of the 9/11 attacks, the United States sought to build the widest international counterterrorism coalition ever assembled, and to delegitimize terrorism in the eyes of the world. Beyond efforts to improve U.S. counterterrorism capabilities at home, and the ability to work with allies on discrete fronts, there has also been a broader attempt to construct a multinational regime to stand steadfast in the battle against al-Qaeda. For a while much was achieved. The sleeping superpower had been struck, and many nations viewed its cause as just. NATO came to the aid of the United States, for the first time in history invoking its bedrock clause of collective defense. Great power relations were recast, for a time, as traditional rivals such as Russia, China, and India found common cause with America against a threat shared by all. The United Nations quickly passed new resolutions denouncing terrorism and dictating mandatory steps that states should take to deny terrorists support or sanctuary.

Indeed, a cornerstone of the Bush administration's coalition-building efforts and attempts to institutionalize a worldwide rejection of terrorism in the weeks following 9/11 was passage of United Nations Resolution 1373. The resolution committed U.N. members to a series of binding steps designed to staunch the lifeblood of terrorist organizations, including freezing terrorist assets, prosecuting or extraditing terrorists themselves, tightening border controls, and issuing national identity papers. The measures enumerated in the resolution are mandatory for all states, a caveat rarely used by the U.N. Security Council, giving the document unique historical significance. The United States also helped establish a special Security Council committee on terrorism to monitor compliance with the resolution. The committee offered financial aid and assistance to governments that were willing to cooperate but lacked the necessary resources and know-how to do so.

"After the 9/11 attacks, President Bush was faced with the challenge of channeling the understandable anger of the American people into an effective counterterrorism policy," said Lee Hamilton.

"Initially, I believe, he did a good job of focusing the public's attention on the 'war on terror' and rallying the international community around U.S. counterterrorism efforts, including the campaign to go after the Taliban and al-Qaeda in Afghanistan. Unfortunately, the administration has not been able to sustain that international support, largely because many nations saw Iraq as unconnected. Bush has always conflated the two, but I have grave doubts about the wisdom of that approach."

The Bush administration's decision to make Iraq the centerpiece in its "war on terror" colors many aspects of the United States's conflict with Islamic extremist terrorism, as this report makes clear in a number of chapters. The bruising diplomacy that preceded the Iraq invasion essentially splintered the broad counterterrorism coalition that coalesced after 9/11. Disagreements over the Iraq War not only paralyzed the U.N. Security Council but also estranged the United States from some of its closest traditional allies—allies that rejected the idea of war in Iraq as a natural outgrowth of the battle against Osama bin Laden. As a bloody guerrilla insurgency and sectarian strife drags on in Iraq more than three years later, much of the early momentum in building an international counterterrorism consensus has been lost.

"Whether you think it was right or wrong to invade Iraq and topple Saddam Hussein's regime, there is little doubt that the Iraq War has alienated much of the world from the United States, and created tremendous distrust in Muslim nations in particular," said Bruce Hoffman. "In that sense, al-Qaeda unleashed a chain of events that achieved in five years what the Soviet Union was unable to accomplish in nearly a half century—namely, splitting the Western alliance and creating fissures between the United States and close allies such as France, Spain, and Germany."

## Return to Multilateralism

Since the Iraq invasion, the Bush administration has worked to repair its bilateral relationships and construct regional counterterrorism coalitions, with varying degrees of success. NATO has elevated counterterrorism operations to a primary mission and taken increased responsibility for military operations in Afghanistan, where a resurgent Taliban continues to contest portions of the country. And as was already noted, even after U.S. relations with many allies soured over Iraq, bilateral counterterrorism intelligence sharing and cooperation continued apace. This is true despite France's public opposition to the Bush administration on the war, and regardless of Spain's withdrawal of troops from Iraq after the Madrid bombings.

The United States has also launched efforts to help weak-but-willing states better police their own territories against encroachment by terrorists, often through military-to-military engagements that include training and equipping indigenous forces. U.S. Special Forces have worked closely with the military in the Philippines, for example, to bolster that army's capabilities in battling the Islamic extremist terrorist groups Abu Sayyaf and the Moro Islamic Liberation Front. Similarly, the United States worked with the military of Georgia to help it clear out an Islamic extremist sanctuary in the Pankisi Gorge. U.S. Central Command has also established operations in Djibouti to block terrorists seeking safe haven in the Horn of Africa, and U.S. European Command has launched a trans-Sahara counterterrorism initiative that involves the training and equipping of security and counterterrorism forces in African nations such as Mali, Mauritania, and Niger.

Part of that outreach has also included building regional counterterrorism coalitions of concerned nations. As part of the trans-Sahara initiative, the U.S. European Command held a series of "chiefs of defense conferences" for military leaders in Africa. A similar "Bali Process" attempted to coordinate regional counterterrorism activities in Asia. As part of that Bali process, the United States, Britain, and Australia have shared intelligence and counterterrorism techniques and technologies with Asian partners.

Despite that progress in international counterterrorism cooperation, however, there is still a sense in Asia and other regions that the United States has too narrowly pursued its own national interest in its global "war on terror," and that the phrase itself fails to capture the nuances of the common terrorist threat. Likewise, animus continues to run deep over the Iraq War and its aftermath, exacerbating the perception of an America intent on unilaterally prosecuting a global war with little regard for international norms or the counsel of traditional allies. In that sense, the Bush administration's post-Iraq fence-mending with U.S. allies remains very much a work in progress. Until those memories fade and Iraq stabilizes, many allies will continue to cast a skeptical eye on U.S. leadership in the fight against Islamic extremist terrorism.

"From a European point of view, I would recommend that the U.S. government refrain from this tendency towards unilateralism and act more on a multilateral or collective basis, because the problem of Islamist terrorism is not going to be solved unilaterally," said Fernando Reinares. "Europeans also still have problems understanding how the invasion of Iraq related to the broader war on terrorism, especially since no linkages were found between Iraq and 9/11, or between Saddam [Hussein] and al-Qaeda. So the credibility of the U.S. government has suffered, and many people believe Washington has given military responses too much prominence in this fight against Islamist terrorism."

Regaining that trust and building sustainable counterterrorism coalitions for what may well prove a generation-spanning conflict will not be easy, but President Bush made a good start when he recently voiced regret for some of his own blunt rhetoric.

"Hopefully the U.S. government has come to realize what it should have known from the start: that all this chest thumping and hubris on display after 9/11—how we were going to take on the terror groups 'one after another,' and countries were either 'with us or against us'—was simplistic and unhelpful," said Brian Jenkins, author of *Unconquerable Nation*. "Counterterrorism requires a multinational approach and international cooperation, not as goals in themselves but, rather, because they are absolute prerequisites to success. Every time you see authorities capture a leading terrorist or uncover a terrorist plot, that's the result of international cooperation, not the consequence of the United States acting unilaterally. So we need to get away from this operative refrain of 'with us or against us' and start building far more complex and tailored counterterrorism coalitions that will require a lot of diplomatic skill to hold together over the long term."

## Outreach to Muslims

The invasion of Iraq and the continued sectarian violence and bloodshed in that country also greatly complicate U.S. outreach to Muslim nations. Images of American troops fighting the Iraqi insurgents, with the often attendant collateral damage of dead Iraqi civilians, have inflamed hostility toward the United States in the Muslim world and on the Arab "street." A widespread perception that the United States backed Israel in its recent bombing campaign in Lebanon only adds to this rampant anti-Americanism.

Yet Osama bin Laden and his fellow extremists are often their own worst enemies when it comes to the willingness of Arab and Muslim governments to participate in the fight against Islamic extremists. Two al-Qaeda-directed assassination attempts on Pervez Musharraf only solidified the Pakistani president's support for the counterterrorism coalition, just as numerous al-Qaeda attacks targeting Saudi Arabian oil-production facilities finally and belatedly spurred the Saudi royal family to take the threat of Islamic terrorism seriously. Suicide bombings in Jordan targeting a wedding party, launched by al-Qaeda in Iraq, likewise significantly reduced sympathy for al-Qaeda in that Muslim country.

"Despite great hostility towards America, the governments in Pakistan and Saudi Arabia are actively cooperating in the fight against al-Qaeda and its allies," said Brian Jenkins. "That doesn't mean they are taking a pro-U.S. stance; it just means they understand that regime survival is at stake, and that the terrorists are targeting their governments specifically."

U.S.-led efforts to pressure state sponsors of terrorism to end their support of Islamic extremist terrorists have also met with mixed results. Libya dropped its support for terrorist groups and abandoned its weapons-of-mass-destruction (WMD) programs as a result of international isolation and Tripoli's own fears of domestic Islamic extremism. On the other hand, the Iranian- and Syrian-backed Islamic terrorist group Hezbollah was integral to the recent warfare in Lebanon, bombing Israel and killing and kidnapping Israeli troops. Hezbollah's reemergence as a key player in the region, and the growing support for its actions among many in the Muslim world, underscored just how short of the mark the U.S.-led "war on terror" has fallen in delegitimizing terrorism or ending state sponsorship.

However, the Islamic extremist terrorism that struck the United States on 9/11—and continues to wreak havoc around the globe in a steady stream of bombings and attacks—is ultimately neither reliant on state sponsorship nor vulnerable to traditional state-to-state pressures. "After 9/11 there was a mistaken belief—evidently held, among others, by some administration officials—that a state had to be involved in the attacks. The rhetoric about an 'axis of evil' focused on states rather than the nonstate terrorists who were really involved," said Paul Pillar. "In fact, one of the biggest evolutions in terrorism over the past twenty years has been the reduction in the role of states. By defining the enemy in this conflict as an axis of states rather than nonstate terrorists, the Bush administration showed that it was stuck in a pre-9/11 mind-set."

Any battle against al-Qaeda and its offshoots will not be decided by the elimination of state sponsorship of terrorism. Yet the support of allies and a widespread coalition remains vital to any successful campaign. Without this support, many opportunities for success will clearly be missed.

## Great Power Relations

In formulating its post-9/11 strategy for winning the global "war on terror," the Bush administration saw an opportunity to recast great power relationships and rivalries within the context of a fight against a common enemy. Russia confronted its own threat from Chechen rebels involved in an ongoing separatist movement, and the administration needed Moscow's acquiescence in establishing U.S. military bases near Afghanistan. China wanted a freer hand to deal with its own Muslim populations and had no reason to directly oppose the U.S.-led fight against Islamic terrorists. India saw an opportunity to reverse its Cold War estrangement from the United States and draw international support for its own fight in the disputed Kashmiri region.

"I do think the Bush administration was fairly successful at recasting great power relations and bringing Russia, China, and India into the 'war on terror,'" said Lee Hamilton. The problem, he noted, is that five years later, the United States continues to make the war on terrorism totally dominant in U.S. foreign policy. "Because we're so focused on terrorism, we have become insensitive to the agendas and interests of other nations. For instance, when President Bush goes to Latin America, he talks about terrorism, but when China's president goes there, he talks about economic development for that region. My point is we have to be more sensitive to the interests and needs of other nations. International relations are too complicated and interconnected to view them strictly with a focus on counterterrorism."

Support for counterterrorism efforts are often best won through less direct means. As the United States and its allies attempt to forge alliances and build coalitions throughout the Middle East, Asia, and Africa, the particulars of each country may be the best path to negotiation and cooperation. Though this may not be where the battle is won or lost, it is certainly integral to what is destined to be a long, drawn-out struggle. ■

# Preventing Terrorist Attack with Nukes, "Dirty Bombs," Germs, and Chemicals

# 4

| | OVERALL GRADE | C |
|---|---|---|

| | |
|---|---|
| Priority given to preventing terrorists from acquiring CBRN | C |
| Effectiveness of international counter-proliferation policies | C |
| Efforts to secure nuclear weapons materials in Russia | B– |
| Efforts to stop CBRN technology transfers | C+ |
| Ability to locate and dismantle nuclear proliferation networks | C |
| Ability to prevent WMD scientists from cooperating with terrorists | C– |
| Attempts to deter North Korea and Iran from acquiring nuclear weapons | D– |
| Effectiveness of the Nuclear Nonproliferation Regime | D |

There is a truism of counterterrorism: The authorities have to be right all the time, while the terrorists only have to be right once. Some terrorist plots will succeed no matter what precautions are taken against them, if for no other reason than the law of averages. Governments cannot protect everything, all at once, all of the time. However, when it comes to preventing a terrorist attack with WMD, and nuclear weapons in particular, the authorities really must be right all the time; the potential impact of such an attack is simply too devastating to countenance.

There is often a great deal of confusion when it comes to the idea of weapons of mass destruction. But when the politicization of the term is tossed aside, we are left with the very real possibility—and still-frightening idea—of terrorists using any form of chemical, biological, nuclear, or radiological material (CBRN) to kill massive numbers of civilians, or at least to unleash a psychologically, and perhaps even economically, devastating attack on our sense of safety, security, and well-being. Any attack using CBRN, even if it did not result in widespread casualties, would likely achieve the terrorists' perennial goal of undermining public confidence in authorities' ability to protect people. So, whether these weapons caused mass destruction or mass disruption, the consequences are liable to far exceed those of any more conventional terrorist attack we have seen before.

Because there is almost no margin of error in preventing a terrorist attack that has the ability to inflict wanton carnage or intense fear, judging efforts in this field of counterterrorism and nonproliferation is highly speculative; much progress may be made, yet one lapse can lead to a deep emotional impact at best, innumerable casualties at worst. Credit must be given for the fact that there has been no such successful unconventional Islamic extremist terrorist attack to date. Yet when near perfection is called for, it is important to consider the likelihood of the threat, and to ask whether the countermeasures taken are sufficient to protect our way of life.

"A nuclear attack by terrorists is the least likely but most consequential potential act of terrorism, because it could literally call into question the ability of a nation to survive," said Lee Hamilton. Al-Qaeda has certainly made clear its desire to acquire a weapon of mass destruction, he noted, and if the terrorists had attacked Manhattan with a nuclear bomb instead of airplanes on 9/11, it might have led to the death of hundreds of thousands of people rather than 3,000. "On the other hand, the obstacles to terrorists acquiring a nuclear weapon are very high, and governments have spent a lot of time and money trying to thwart this nexus of terrorism and WMD. My bottom line is that this is a threat we can do something about, and we still haven't elevated it high enough on our list of counterterrorism priorities."

The difficulty of gauging the response to a threat that has not occurred, but which can easily conjure doomsday scenarios, was reflected in differing opinions among members of the Council on Global Terrorism on whether or not governments have done enough to keep the threat at bay.

"The danger posed by terrorism and weapons of mass destruction is not one that lends itself to clear analysis by trend lines, since just one incident will be one too many," said Paul Pillar. "The issue of terrorists potentially acquiring nuclear or other unconventional weapons has been such a concern for so long, however, that I would say it has even received disproportionate attention relative to other potential terrorist threats."

There has been a lot of unhelpful duplication of effort in the government bureaucracy, said Pillar, as each agency involved in counterterrorism and nonproliferation has established its own unit to thwart the danger of nuclear terrorism in particular. "Meanwhile, one of the major lessons of 9/11 was that you don't need exotic weapons to have a truly catastrophic impact. I wouldn't be surprised if there were a London-type suicide bombing attack on our metros tomorrow, or a Washington sniper scenario that paralyzes our cities. My point is that it doesn't take a weapon of mass destruction for a terrorist attack to inflict an awful lot of damage."

This remains one of the key distinctions in the debate over CBRN—the threat that terrorists may turn these materials into weapons of mass destruction and the idea that even a conventional attack could prove as deadly, if not more so. One thing that we know for sure, however, is that a traditional Cold War–type nuclear bomb successfully detonated by a terrorist group would lead to an innumerable number of deaths.

## Terrorists Seeking Nuclear Bombs and Materials

The trend of Islamic extremist terrorists seeking WMD and hoping to inflict wanton destruction and carnage is clear and worrisome. The conventional wisdom that terrorists are more interested in publicity for their cause than mass casualties began to change in the 1990s. Religiously inspired terrorists with an apocalyptic worldview, neither beholden to nor constrained by state sponsors, began to display a thirst for killing civilians in large numbers going back at least to the 1993 attempted attack on the World Trade Center. The Islamic terrorists involved in that incident aimed to topple one tower into the other in hopes of killing 250,000 people.

Meanwhile, Osama bin Laden's desire to add nuclear weapons to al-Qaeda's arsenal is well documented. In 1998, bin Laden issued a proclamation titled "The Nuclear Bomb of Islam," declaring that "it is the duty of Muslims to prepare as much force as possible to terrorize the enemies of God." Later that year, bin Laden told an interviewer that acquiring weapons of mass destruction was a "religious duty" for Muslims.

Bin Laden was not engaging in idle rhetoric. During the 1990s, senior al-Qaeda operatives tried repeatedly to buy enriched uranium, an essential ingredient in nuclear weapons. Two Pakistani nuclear scientists met with bin Laden and his top lieutenants in 2001 for three days of discussions on WMD, including radiological "dirty bombs." CNN reporters rummaging through an al-Qaeda safe house in Kabul in 2002 found a twenty-five-page document containing designs for a nuclear weapon. As recently as this spring, top U.S. intelligence officials stated publicly that they continue to disrupt al-Qaeda attempts to acquire WMD.

## Nuclear Proliferation

The spread of nuclear weapons and related technologies are also pointing in the wrong direction. The Bush administration has done little to bolster the Nuclear Non-Proliferation Treaty (NPT) regime—the international bulwark against the spread of nuclear weapons—since it began to fray with the nuclear-weapons tests of both India and Pakistan in 1998. Recently, President Bush announced a civilian nuclear-energy deal that many experts predict will allow India to vastly increase the size of its nuclear arsenal, despite the fact that India has not ratified the treaty. Pakistan, a fellow outlier and the likely home to many fugitive al-Qaeda operatives, responded by announcing its own planned increase in the production of nuclear fissile material.

In other negative news, U.S. intelligence agencies successfully broke up the nuclear smuggling ring of Pakistani scientist A.Q. Khan, but not before his agents reportedly helped advance the nuclear programs of North Korea and Iran, both profound proliferation risks. Pakistan's continued refusal to let U.S. agents interrogate Khan has made it impossible to determine the full extent of the damage inflicted by his nuclear black market.

In its first term, the Bush administration dumped North Korea and Iran into an "axis of evil" and adopted a stance of no direct negotiations combined with threats of "regime change" in an effort to force both nations to abandon their suspected nuclear-weapons programs. In response, these states appear to have accelerated their nuclear programs, providing a deterrent to U.S. military force and worsening the crises. More recently, the administration moved to multilateral talks in hopes of a better outcome. Iran's nuclear program was recently referred to the U.N. Security Council, and the possibility of sanctions looms.

Despite these efforts, the campaign to arrest the nuclear ambitions and programs of both North Korea and Iran must be judged a failure. Iran continues on its path of uranium enrichment and, by some estimates, may be within five years of producing a nuclear bomb.

Most nuclear experts believe that North Korea already has several nuclear weapons, and that it likely has increased the size of its arsenal in recent years.

"The specter of Iran armed with nuclear weapons casts an especially long shadow over the entire discussion of terrorism and WMD," said Walter Reich. "Given the nature of the Iranian regime, the prospect of them acquiring a nuclear weapon and perhaps passing it to terrorists may well be even more ominous than the leakage of fissile material from the former Soviet Union."

Despite Iran's continued close ties to the Islamic terrorist group Hezbollah, some experts doubt that Tehran would actually risk passing a nuclear weapon to such an unpredictable proxy. "The threat that a regime might pass a nuclear weapon to terrorists was used as a justification for invading Iraq, and similar rhetoric is now raised over Iran, but there is a substantial historical record that suggests that even some very nasty regimes—such as that of Saddam Hussein and the former Soviet Union—never passed weapons of mass destruction to terrorists," said Paul Pillar. "When you sit down to analyze the threat, there are not a lot of incentives for states to risk relinquishing such weapons to terrorists."

## Fissile Material and Dirty Bombs

Short of acquiring an actual nuclear weapon from a state, al-Qaeda or other terrorist groups could potentially attain a nuclear capability by gaining access to nuclear fissile material and then fashioning it into a crude nuclear device. These dirty bombs use nuclear fissile material in conjunction with conventional explosives to disperse radiological material. Members of the Council on Global Terrorism believe that while the use of a nuclear weapon by a terrorist group remains the least likely and most dangerous threat, a radiological or dirty bomb is of far greater likelihood and would still have a profound impact.

In interrogations with his captors, a Pakistani scientist who met with Osama bin Laden in 2001 reported that al-Qaeda had already acquired some nuclear material from a jihadi group in Uzbekistan, and the scientist admitted telling bin Laden and his lieutenants how the material could be fashioned into a dirty bomb. The need only for the material, rather than a full-fledged bomb, makes the possibility of attack with this type of device most worrisome.

Partly for that reason, the U.S. government has spent years, and billions of dollars, on cooperative threat-reduction programs designed to secure the vast stockpiles of nuclear fissile material in Russia and other nations of the former Soviet Union. These measures have done much, and the situation is far better than before. Yet significant amounts of fissile material stockpiles remain inadequately accounted for and secured.

"We know that the bulk of the nuclear fissile material is in the former Soviet Union, and we know that as recently as a few years ago some of that nuclear material was protected by the equivalent of a chain-link fence and a padlock that you might use to lock up a bicycle," said Lee Hamilton. "That's why I was part of a Department of Energy commission that recommended increasing what we spend on cooperative threat-reduction programs from $1 billion to $3 billion annually. Even now the Russians don't know exactly how much nuclear material they have, and not nearly enough has been done to secure those vulnerable stockpiles."

The threat of nuclear fissile material leaking from the former Soviet Union and being used in terrorist attacks especially concerns officials in Europe, given their territorial continuity with Russia and Moscow's former satellites. Adding to Russian vulnerabilities, the specter of nuclear proliferation in the Middle East and Pakistan's nuclear program only increase the threat; both regions provide easy access into Europe. "The danger of leaked fissile material being used in a dirty bomb is very clear to us in Europe," said Fernando Reinares. "There is a lot of literature about such dirty bombs on jihadist Web sites that we monitor and prominent al-Qaeda ideologues and strategists have strongly advocated its use."

In reviewing the entire issue of nuclear terrorism, French officials also concluded that the threat of a dirty bomb was perhaps the most plausible. "The most realistic scenario we came up with was that terrorists hijack radioactive materials that come from Russia each week and are used in cancer-research centers in Paris," said Xavier Raufer. "If that radioactive material were combined with a stick of dynamite, and a dirty bomb were set off at Place de la Concorde, depending on the prevailing winds, it could make a two-square-kilometer stretch of Paris uninhabitable for twenty or thirty years. So now the French army escorts that shipment of material each week."

Raufer noted that despite the obvious dangers, to date there have been no actual incidents of smuggled nuclear fissile material reaching the hands of terrorists. "It's worth noting that all the published intercepts of fissile material up to this time have been the result of sting operations by police or intelligence services," he said. "Not once have we intercepted a shipment actually bound for a terrorist group."

## Biological and Chemical Weapons

Befitting Osama bin Laden's tendency to leave no stone unturned in searching for new and unconventional ways to strike at the United States, al-Qaeda is also known to have a keen interest in developing biological and chemical weapons. Short of a nuclear explosion or the use of a dirty bomb that could scatter radiological material over widespread surrounding areas, there remains the chance that terrorists will use other CBRN agents in an attempt to forge a weapon to kill vastly and indiscriminately. In an intercepted memo, al-Qaeda's second in command, Ayman al-Zawahiri, wrote to Muhammad Atef, a now-deceased al-Qaeda lieutenant, expressing his thoughts on the utility of biological weapons in particular. Citing articles published in *The New England Journal of Medicine* and *The Journal of Immunology*, as well as books such as *Peace or Pestilence* and *Chemical Warfare*, al-Zawahiri noted that the destructive power of biological weapons "was no less than that of nuclear weapons," and that a "germ attack is often detected days after it occurs, which raises the number of victims" and makes defense against such weapons "very difficult."

Once again, al-Qaeda's leaders were not engaging in empty talk or mere speculation. Yazid Sufaat, a U.S.-trained microbiologist and former captain in the Malaysian army, was recruited to the extremist cause, working through the al-Qaeda-affiliated group Jemaah Islamiyah. Sufaat set up shop at an al-Qaeda camp near Kandahar, Afghanistan, where his efforts reportedly focused on the weaponization of anthrax. Sufaat was arrested in late 2001, but it's worth noting that when 9/11 mastermind Khalid Sheikh Mohammed was apprehended two years later, he was staying in the Rawalpindi home of a Pakistani bacteriologist who has since disappeared.

The focus on weaponizing anthrax, and the closure of the U.S. House of Representatives and numerous U.S. Senate offices during the turmoil of October 2001, ushered in a new and ominous chapter in the annals of bioterrorism. Previously, the only proven incidence of bioterrorism in the United States occurred in 1984, when a religious cult in Oregon spread salmonella at restaurant salad bars to sway a local election. Although 750 people fell ill, the incident seemed more bizarre than apocalyptic.

By contrast, the anthrax that arrived by letter in the office of the Senate majority leader in October of 2001 was a potent, finely milled variety, consisting of particles so miniscule that they spread through the air without detection. Eventually, more than thirty Senate staffers tested positive for exposure to anthrax from that single envelope and piece of paper, some in adjacent offices. If such a pure form of anthrax had been coupled with an efficient dispersal device such as an aerosol spray, and the attack not telegraphed with a crude note, the ensuing death toll could have been significant. Confidence is certainly not inspired by the fact that the source of such a dangerous biological-warfare agent has never been determined.

In keeping with its touch-all-bases approach, al-Qaeda also ran a training camp in Afghanistan that specialized in teaching operatives how to produce chemical-warfare agents. In 2003, al-Qaeda operatives were reportedly within forty-five days of mounting an attack on the New York City subway system with lethal cyanide gas—and the track record does not end there. Earlier this year, British authorities possessed strong evidence suggesting that a suicide bomber was preparing to launch an attack in London using a "chemical vest," a device that would allow the terrorist to strap toxic agents to his chest and release them at the opportune moment.

These purported attempted chemical attacks, or at least the ideas for them, were presaged by the 1995 sarin nerve gas plot of the Japanese religious cult Aum Shinrikyo, which killed twelve people and wounded 3,796 others. There were reports at the time that the cult planned to carry out a similar attack in the United States. Once again, if the sarin nerve gas had been coupled with a more efficient dispersal device, the death toll inflicted by Aum Shinrikyo might have been far greater.

"In terms of mind-set, al-Qaeda's leaders have talked publicly about their legitimate right to and justification for killing 4 million Americans, including 2 million children, as retaliation for our supposed outrages against Muslims," said Brian Jenkins. "So I have little doubt that if their experiments with biological or chemical weapons were to produce an actual weapon of mass destruction, al-Qaeda would use it. Fortunately, their unconventional weapons capabilities significantly trail their ambitions. Even if some of their plots to use such weapons had not been foiled, I doubt the resultant casualties would rise to the level of an actual weapon of mass destruction."

In an era of globalization where epidemics can spread around the world in forty-eight hours, a biological weapon is also a double-edged sword that is at least as likely to cut the hand that wields it. "Even if al-Qaeda or a similar group were able to unleash a deadly contagion like smallpox in the United States, our health-care system would eventually contain the epidemic," said Jenkins. "When it inevitably spreads around the planet and hits Cairo and Karachi, however, the death toll on Muslims could look like the Black Plague in the Middle Ages."

## Lines of Defense

As a secondary line of defense against the spread of WMD or related materials, the United States has successfully formed a broad nonproliferation coalition under the umbrella of the Proliferation Security Initiative. More than sixty nations are now signed on to a program that tracks and intercepts suspected shipments of WMD and related technologies and materials, whether in transit on the high seas or through the air. The Department of Homeland Security is also initiating programs whereby cargo bound for the United States is screened for nuclear or WMD-related materials before leaving overseas ports. As a last line of defense, the United States is developing nuclear-detection devices for American ports that do not require containers to be searched by hand.

While taking note of those added defenses, the Council on Global Terrorism believes that five years after 9/11, the United States should be further along in developing reliable detection protocols, and views with concern trends that may make a terrorist attack with unconventional weapons more likely in the future. The Islamic extremist terrorists who struck the United States have backed up their stated desire for such weapons with attempts to acquire them. The apocalyptic vision and hatred that inspired the indiscriminate carnage of 9/11 has spread, and the technology underlying these doomsday weapons continues to proliferate.

"Even a limited terrorist attack involving an unconventional radiological, chemical, or biological weapon could have enormous psychological consequences, generating unprecedented fear and alarm," said Bruce Hoffman. A key lesson from the October 2001 anthrax letters, he said, was that terrorists don't have to kill thousands of people to create panic and foment fear and insecurity. "Killing five people with a biological-warfare agent under very mysterious conditions was quite effective in unnerving the entire nation. Our challenge is thus to prepare adequately for an uncertain threat that might have profound consequences, and at the same time to avoid overreaction." ■

# Protecting the U.S. Homeland

5

| | OVERALL GRADE | C |
|---|---|---|

| | |
|---|---|
| Effectiveness of the Department of Homeland Security | C– |
| Increasing aviation security | B– |
| Improving cargo screening | C– |
| Protecting U.S. borders | D+ |
| Improving the ability to track potential terrorists/ dangerous cargo traveling by air and sea | C– |
| Protecting critical infrastructure | C– |
| Increasing the security of mass transit | D– |
| Preventing cyber attack | D+ |
| Improving emergency response to terrorist attack | D+ |

n the immediate aftermath of September 11, 2001, few counterterrorism experts would have predicted that five years later the U.S. homeland would remain free of another attack. Osama bin Laden had already spent a decade meticulously honing al-Qaeda's capabilities. Tens of thousands of Islamic extremists had passed through terrorist training camps in Afghanistan. Given the organization's modus operandi, it seemed likely that follow-up attacks were in the pipeline. For all U.S. authorities knew, there were al-Qaeda sleeper cells inside the nation ready to strike.

The fact that the United States has not suffered another attack on its homeland is in large measure a testament to an extraordinary mobilization of national will and American power. U.S. military, intelligence, and law-enforcement services took the offensive against al-Qaeda in Afghanistan and around the world. In the largest reorganization of the government in half a century, the administration and Congress bolstered defenses by consolidating multiple federal agencies, border controls, transportation securities, and emergency responses into a new Department of Homeland Security, and military defenses into a new Northern Command.

After nearly a decade of al-Qaeda striking U.S. interests without a commensurate response, such a massive mobilization and restructuring was an important signal of national determination and resolve. "The government's response to the 9/11 attacks showed that we as a nation were ready to really transform ourselves and dare large tasks in order to meet this new threat of global terrorism, and in principle that sent an important message," said Walter Reich. "If you look back in history, we responded similarly to other seminal threats."

At the beginning of World War II, he noted, America threw off its self-imposed isolation and mobilized and reorganized to cope with the global threat of fascism, becoming a superpower in the process. "We responded with a similar massive reorganization during the Cold War to counter the threat of communism, in the process spending hundreds of billions of dollars developing a nuclear deterrent. Now, after 9/11, we are again retooling our government to deal with the threat of global terrorism. And despite reports of wasteful spending and problems at the Department of Homeland Security, I think we've shown an important impetus in rethinking every sphere of our government. The reorganizations for World War II and the Cold War were likewise problematic and wasted a lot of money. They were also necessary."

Despite that ambitious reorganization, the U.S. homeland has remained free of another terrorist attack in large measure due to good fortune. As both the 9/11 and Robb-Silverman commissions reported, there are still persistent vulnerabilities in U.S. defenses. History suggests that al-Qaeda and associated Islamic extremist terrorist groups are analyzing those defenses and vulnerabilities, and shaping their plots accordingly.

"I believe the reorganization under the Department of Homeland Security was the right thing to do, but such major government reorganizations are always difficult, and they create a lot of problems in the near term. You never get as far in fixing the problem as you intended," said Lee Hamilton. "In general, my view of homeland security is that we are still not treating it with sufficient urgency, and we have yet to get our priorities straight. We talk about the hard choices between what to protect and what not to protect, but we don't make them. And despite our good work and great fortune in avoiding another attack on the homeland, I believe we will be hit again."

## Homeland Security

In many ways the post-9/11 story of shoring up the U.S. homeland's defenses is one of two steps forward and one step back. For instance, more stringent screening of airline passengers and luggage by the new Transportation Security Administration (TSA), combined with reinforced cockpit doors in commercial aircraft and an increase in onboard air marshals, make the probability of another 9/11-type hijacking more remote. New air patrols and awareness of the threat by U.S. Northern Command make it less likely that a hijacked aircraft would reach its intended target; a vulnerability cruelly exposed by 9/11 has been at least partially addressed.

Yet numerous independent reports on the Department of Homeland Security have revealed just how much remains to be done even in the realm of air security. The TSA's terrorist watch list remains incomplete and deeply flawed, resulting in the frequent detention of passengers with names similar to those of suspected terrorists. Despite spending an estimated $130 million on a Secure Flight program that was supposed to expedite screening for frequent fliers and protect innocent travelers while focusing on terrorists, the TSA shelved the program for reassessment earlier this year, and has yet to indicate when it will be reintroduced. The recently foiled terrorist plot to down jetliners over the Atlantic revealed that the TSA had taken little precaution against the ingredients of liquid bombs being smuggled aboard planes, even though these weapons figured prominently in a thwarted al-Qaeda attack in the mid-1990s.

Of perhaps still greater concern was the finding of the Robb-Silverman commission regarding intelligence failures that persist post-9/11. The commission determined that the Department of Homeland Security "has faced immense challenges . . . in all four roles it plays in the intelligence community—as collector, analyst, disseminator, and customer." This raises the unsettling possibility that the department most directly responsible for defending the homeland from another terrorist plot may be unable to uphold its mission.

"Despite all the well-known difficulties in getting DHS organized and the remaining vulnerabilities people write about, homeland security has received orders-of-magnitude more attention than it did prior to 9/11, and because of that we are better off on the defensive side of the terrorism equation," said Paul Pillar. "Unfortunately there are clear limits to what we can achieve through defensive security measures. Couple those limits with the inherent difficulty of acquiring actionable intelligence on terrorist plots, magnify it because the threat is becoming more diffuse with the dispersion of al-Qaeda and the increase in homegrown Islamist terrorist cells, and the conclusion

I reach is we shouldn't be surprised if the U.S. homeland is struck tomorrow."

The progress of the Department of Homeland Security is simply less than stellar. The department's decision to award less money to both New York and Washington, D.C., in its most recent round of antiterrorism grants raises serious questions about whether the department's classified risk-assessment formula is based on accurate and reliable information or if the system is simply politicized.

In terms of port security and cargo screening, the evaluation of U.S. efforts is equally sobering. The holes in the U.S. Customs and Border Protection cargo-screening system became blatantly clear earlier this year, when twenty-two Chinese stowaways hidden in a container made it all the way to the Port of Seattle. The advanced X-ray technology that may one day make it possible to scan each of the estimated 11 million cargo containers that enter the United States annually is still years away. Only about half of those containers are currently subject to even a radiation scan that can detect nuclear materials—a dangerous vulnerability Congress indicated must be plugged. A truly global system for inspecting and sealing containers at their port of origin, and then monitoring them in transit, is still in its concept development and experimentation phase.

Meanwhile, five years after 9/11, the Department of Homeland Security only recently announced that it would begin checking the names of port workers against terrorist watch lists and immigration databases. A program to create forge-proof biometric identification cards for all transportation workers is still only in the testing phase. Both the U.S. Coast Guard and Navy have also publicly acknowledged that their abilities to accurately identify and track small ships around U.S. shores—or what is known as "maritime domain awareness"—are woefully insufficient.

U.S. efforts to enlist the private sector in strengthening homeland security are also lacking. The Department of Homeland Security has been slow to establish and enforce mandatory standards for security of critical infrastructure such as chemical plants, despite the fact that a terrorist attack on some of these structures could literally threaten tens of thousands of Americans.

"In terms of protecting critical infrastructure, the government has done a poor job of determining what the private and public sectors are each responsible for, and who pays for what," said Lee Hamilton. "In many cases, the big corporations are already way ahead of the government in terms of security. What you have to worry about are the middle-sized companies that run small plants or transport chemicals and who may skimp on security as a way to save money. Yet if that critical infrastructure is attacked, it could lead to the death of a lot more than 3,000 people."

## Emergency Response

The chaotic government response last year to Hurricane Katrina and the flooding of New Orleans also revealed just how far the U.S. government has to go in honing its emergency-response capabilities. Katrina was just the type of "incident of national consequence" that might be expected if the nation were struck by a terrorist attack with WMD, and the results of the relief effort were sobering. U.S. Northern Command adopted what many observers felt was an overly passive posture in the week before Katrina made landfall, despite much that was known about the vulnerability of New Orleans's levee system. The Federal Emergency Management Agency was terribly unprepared for a disaster of such proportions. Federal, state, and local authorities feuded bitterly in the days after the hurricane hit over the fundamental issue of who was in charge.

Perhaps most disturbing, federal, state, and local emergency responders lacked a basic necessity: an interoperable communications system to talk with one another and establish at least a modicum of "situational awareness"—a deficiency already highlighted by the 9/11 commission more than two years ago. Given its past practices, there is also little doubt that al-Qaeda and affiliated terrorist groups were looking at the U.S. government's response to Hurricane Katrina and taking copious notes.

"Because of the tremendous amount of money spent on homeland security since 9/11, there's a widespread assumption that we're much better prepared in terms of responding to a crisis, but Hurricane Katrina tested that assumption, and the results did not inspire confidence," said Bruce Hoffman. "We've seen numerous reports of homeland-security grants going to buy air-conditioned garbage trucks and security cameras for small Alaskan towns, and here we find out that our emergency responders in a major U.S. city still lacked the radios to talk to each other, and federal, state, and local officials have yet to fix their coordination problems. I would have hoped we learned those lessons on 9/11."

Another lesson that has yet to filter adequately through the homeland-security community, he added, was the great vulnerability of mass-transit systems, especially in large urban areas. In the terrorist bombings of Madrid and London, a similar vulnerability was cruelly exploited at the cost of hundreds of innocent lives. "I think it's interesting that after 9/11 we developed a very low threshold of risk in terms of aviation, but even after Madrid and London, we still haven't taken concrete steps to better secure mass transit," said Hoffman. "Given that trains are a relatively soft target when compared to commercial airplanes, I find that difficult to explain."

## Border Security

As the recent heated debate in Washington revealed, the issue of border security has become irreversibly intertwined with illegal immigration. Proponents of stricter border protections argue for construction of more barriers along the U.S. border with Mexico, and an increase in the roughly 10,000 border-patrol agents already stationed there. They point out that it is impossible to seal the border against terrorists: 6 million illegal immigrants were apprehended over the last five years alone—one can only imagine the countless numbers that have entered the country undetected.

Yet few lawmakers have suggested increasing the roughly 1,000 agents or border protections along the 4,000-mile border with

Canada, even though that northern line may represent a greater infiltration threat by Islamic extremist terrorists. The Royal Mounted Police recently arrested seventeen alleged Islamic terrorists for plotting a bombing and killing spree. Earlier, U.S. border-patrol agents thwarted a plan by Islamic extremists to blow up Los Angeles International Airport when they searched the bomber's car as it crossed the U.S.-Canadian border—both clear indicators of U.S. vulnerability from the north.

"I think border security is now a legitimate part of the immigration debate, because illegal immigration does have national-security implications," said Lee Hamilton. "The chief aim should be to make sure that every person who crosses our borders is whoever he or she says they are. At the same time, we should also keep in mind that none of the 9/11 hijackers slipped across the border in the dead of night. They generally entered the country legally." Each avenue of protection has its limits.

## Empowering Americans

In the post-9/11 rush to shore up homeland defenses, the U.S. government may also have undervalued the single most effective counterterrorism action of that fateful day. After immigration officials failed to flag 9/11 hijackers for overstaying their visas, and U.S. intelligence and law-enforcement officials failed to connect the dots and penetrate the terrorists' plot, one final defense stood between the hijackers of United Flight 93 and its intended target in Washington, D.C.: a group of ordinary American citizens. Bystanders unwilling to act as fodder in a terrorist outrage against their own country, that small group of passengers took action, launching the only successful counterattack on September 11, 2001.

"The U.S. government gets credit for the fact that we have not suffered another attack on the homeland, but I think we made a fundamental error in homeland security by casting it in terms of gates, guards, and better border protection," said Brian Jenkins. Apart from admonishments to be vigilant, he said, the government completely failed to enlist the American people in the counterterrorism campaign by drawing on deep American traditions of self-reliance, courage, resiliency, and a willingness to come to the aid of neighbors.

"To the contrary, the Bush administration essentially heightened people's anxiety by consigning them to the role of bystanders and telling them to step aside while the government asserted all this executive authority in order to take care of the problem. Rather than appealing to people's fears and worse instincts, I think a more edifying approach would be to appeal to their courage, toughness, and sense of community. We missed an important opportunity to shore up those traditions."

One component of such an appeal to American virtues would be educating the public about the actual risks of terrorism, in contrast to the fear it inspires. Even accounting for those who perished in the 9/11 attacks, the average American in the last five years had about a 1-in-500,000 chance of being killed in an act of terrorism. By contrast, the same person had a 1-in-18,000 chance of dying in a homicide, and a 1-in-9,000 chance of dying in an automobile accident.

"I think the American public needs to be psychologically prepared for future acts of terrorism both large and small, because it is almost inevitable that there will be more bombings such as we saw in London, Madrid, and Mumbai," said Council member Walter Reich. "Just as the British responded with steely determination during the Battle of Britain to the constant German bombings, so too must Americans prepare to respond to terrorist acts. We need to gird ourselves for more, and resolve ourselves that we will survive and not give up." ∎

# Balancing Security and Core Values

# 6

OVERALL
GRADE **D+**

| | |
|---|---|
| Balance between expanded U.S. counterterrorism authority and respect for civil liberties | D |
| Appropriateness of domestic intelligence gathering in the U.S. | D+ |
| Balance between due process and extraordinary threats | D+ |
| Balance between international law and national security concerns | D– |
| Balance between intelligence gathering through coercive interrogation and respecting commitments against torture | D– |
| Balance struck on these issues by partners in counterterrorism | D+ |

After the nation was attacked on September 11, 2001, the United States really did face a war unlike any other in its history. A terrorist group, acting independently of any nation-state, struck a strategic blow to the U.S. homeland by killing more people than Japan's surprise attack on Pearl Harbor. For a time, the attacks paralyzed virtually all air traffic into and out of the United States, and they shook both the economy and the American psyche. The perpetrators were men who wore no uniform and plotted in the shadows, protected by the fundamentalist Islamic Taliban in Afghanistan, a national government in name only.

The Bush administration's response to those unprecedented circumstances, perhaps most understandable in the chaotic weeks and months following 9/11, was to declare war—and then unilaterally disregard many laws and international norms that traditionally govern the enterprise. Detainees swept up in the Afghanistan dragnet were sent to a U.S. military base at Guantánamo Bay, Cuba, beyond the reach of international or domestic law. The administration insisted that the Geneva Conventions on the treatment of prisoners of war did not apply.

High-level al-Qaeda plotters were reportedly held in a secret prison system whose very existence remains classified. "Torture" was redefined by the executive branch to include only those techniques that threaten major organ failure. Suspected terrorists were thus subjected to harsh interrogation methods that supposedly included mock execution by drowning through the technique of "water boarding," whereby a prisoner is tied down with his head lower than his feet while water is poured onto a cloth that covers his mouth. Other severe procedures, like threatening naked prisoners with attack dogs, migrated to the Abu Ghraib prison run by the U.S. military in Iraq. Though many abuses were unauthorized, and the individuals involved have been prosecuted, there was already a pattern and precedent set that encouraged this behavior. The United States also continues to conduct "extraordinary renditions," wherein suspected terrorists are captured or kidnapped and handed over to third-party nations, many of which have abysmal prisoner-treatment track records themselves.

"In the aftermath of 9/11, the United States was thrust into uncharted territory, and it was understandable that we initially had enormous difficulty confronting this preeminent security threat posed by a nonstate actor," said Bruce Hoffman. "Five years later, however, it's become clear that the United States has prosecuted the global 'war on terror' in a way that has widened into a chasm the fissures between the West and Islam, between the United States and its allies, and between U.S. actions and the very values we claim to stand for and advance. Rather than contain the problem, our treatment of detainees at Guantánamo Bay and Abu Ghraib have exacerbated Islamic extremist terrorism by giving our opponents a propaganda bonanza in terms of recruitment and radicalization."

Even after Congress finally intervened and passed a bill banning "cruel and unusual treatment" of U.S. detainees, President Bush signed the bill but claimed presidential exception to the newly enacted restrictions on torture—an assertion of presidential authority to pick and choose which parts of the legislation to honor. President Bush has pursued this right more aggressively and broadly than any of his predecessors.

The administration's actions and declarations of executive power domestically have proven equally aggressive. American citizens charged with collusion with al-Qaeda have been declared "enemy combatants" and held in military prisons for more than three years without due process or access to lawyers or their families. In launching a secret domestic wiretapping program, the administration also claimed executive power to ignore the Foreign Intelligence Surveillance Act, which holds that such wiretaps must be reviewed and approved by a special Foreign Intelligence Surveillance Court.

Likewise, when the Justice Department's Office of Professional Responsibility complied with congressional requests and attempted to review the propriety of the domestic electronic-surveillance program, the White House thwarted the investigation by refusing to give the Justice Department's lawyers the required security clearances.

After the secret prison system for captured al-Qaeda suspects and the domestic wiretapping program were both revealed in newspaper reports, Attorney General Alberto Gonzales took the unusual step of publicly threatening to prosecute the newspapers and send journalists to prison for revealing classified information.

"I believe the U.S. government has been reckless in adopting very aggressive counterterrorism measures, and ignoring numerous rules and international norms, without paying nearly enough attention to finding the right balance between our security and core values such as respect for human rights and civil liberties," said Paul Pillar. "Even if you focus narrowly on counterterrorism, there is clear evidence that some of the coercive interrogation techniques we adopted have backfired by inducing prisoners to say what they thought the interrogator wanted to hear, rather than telling the truth. There's also no question in my mind that our treatment of detainees has damaged the U.S. image overseas in a way that plays into the hostile propaganda of the extremists. In terms of counterterrorism, these policies have simply been counterproductive."

## A Rising Backlash

Increasingly, Congress and the Supreme Court have sought to rein in what both institutions judged to be executive-branch excesses in the global "war on terror." Despite a threatened veto and aggressive lobbying by Vice President Dick Cheney, ninety senators voted for the bill sponsored by Republican John McCain of Arizona banning cruel and inhumane treatment of U.S. detainees. Under Senate pressure the Bush administration has also indicated its possible willingness to submit the domestic wiretapping program to the Foreign Intelligence Surveillance Court after all.

In another blow to and admonishment of the administration's handling of U.S. values in the face of war, the Supreme Court, in its recent historic decision of *Hamdan* v. *Rumsfeld,* ruled that the administration had exceeded its authority in unilaterally deciding whether and how detainees accused of war crimes could be tried in military tribunals. The court also found that the administration was indeed bound by the Geneva Conventions barring cruel and inhumane treatment of prisoners of war. This follows on the heels of the earlier *Hamdi* v. *Rumsfeld* case, wherein the Supreme Court rejected the idea that the president, by simply designating an American an enemy combatant, could deny a U.S. citizen due process or access to a judicial hearing.

"In the period after a disaster like the 9/11 attacks, people are prepared to give up a lot of their civil liberties and right to privacy in order to feel more physically safe," said Walter Reich. "In an open society like ours, however, there's always going to be a vigorous debate about whether we've struck the right balance between protecting ourselves and protecting our core values. As time passes without another successful attack, people gradually start to focus less on physical protection and more on core values. By essentially overturning the Bush administration's detainee policies, the Supreme Court indicated that the pendulum is now swinging back in that direction. I see that shifting and rebalancing back and forth as an inevitable process for a free society facing a seminal threat."

By placing the issue of how to try detainees presently held at Guantánamo Bay squarely before the Congress and the administration, the Supreme Court has given the United States a chance to turn an important corner. Five years into what will likely prove a long conflict against Islamic extremist terrorism, the country still lacks a coherent strategy for dealing with captives. It remains unclear what set of calculations determine whether a detainee is sent to Guantánamo Bay, held in the CIA's secret prison system, tried in domestic U.S. courts, incarcerated in Iraq, or remanded to a third nation. Equally ambiguous is the question of whether the overriding goal of detaining suspects is the extraction of intelligence, their removal from the battlefield for the duration of the conflict, punishment for their actions, or formal prosecution and potential rehabilitation. Furthermore, it is uncertain whether the balance struck between those competing agendas is consistent with international legal norms and U.S. core values.

To date, the United Nations, the International Red Cross, numerous human-rights organizations, and the United States's closest allies have spoken with a single voice in arguing that U.S. detainee treatment in the global war on terrorism has fallen outside acceptable international norms—indeed, that it is an affront to the values America purports to champion.

"The Bush administration seems to view the Supreme Court's decision on detainees as a setback, but in my view it's a major opportunity to really take a strategic view of the entire issue of how to deal with captives in this long struggle," said Brian Jenkins. Even nations with hard-nosed reputations such as Singapore, Saudi Arabia, and Yemen, he said, have launched creative programs to reeducate and rehabilitate Islamic extremists in their prisons, in some cases even working with families of captives so that they are less likely to return to jihad upon release. "We need to create a system for dealing with detainees that is viewed as fair and has broad authority, not simply to incarcerate people indefinitely but also to reward cooperation, induce defections from the extremist ranks, and rehabilitate those that can be brought back to the mainstream."

## Change in Course

The overwhelming passage of legislation banning cruel and inhumane treatment of prisoners, and the Supreme Court's decision that the Geneva Conventions do indeed apply to detainees held at Guantánamo Bay, will also hopefully put to rest an unfortunate debate in the country about the efficacy of torture. To have high-ranking U.S. officials argue against constraints on torture, or to play word games by defining "torture" so narrowly as to make such constraints meaningless, has done great and lasting damage to the reputation of the United States.

Interrogations are, by their nature, obviously stressful and extremely unpleasant affairs. Yet when torture is used, these interrogations move into the realm of the morally reprehensible, and there is ample evidence that torture does not work as a method of extracting reliable information. That any American official would become its advocate in the long run becomes not only unconscionable but also shortsighted.

"After 9/11 and operations in Afghanistan, the U.S. government was faced with a short-term problem of what to do with these unconventional detainees, but we fell into a lasting system of detaining and interrogating people in such a way that the downside has come to far outweigh the benefits," said Paul Pillar. "Maintaining a worldwide gulag system was bound to lead to the kind of excesses we witnessed with Abu Ghraib, and that has greatly damaged our image abroad and in the Muslim world."

In a similar vein, congressional pressure on the administration to submit its domestic wiretapping program to the Foreign Intelligence Surveillance Court will hopefully signal a return to vigorous congressional oversight as a check on executive power in the war against terrorism. That is not to suggest that the wiretapping program itself was ill-advised or necessarily an affront to Americans' inherent right to privacy. Rather, in a nation founded on the rule of law and separation of powers, such programs should be thoroughly vetted so that the right balance between security and core values can be struck.

"I think the president can make a good case that he needs to conduct surveillance on suspected terrorists in a way that Americans traditionally might find intrusive, and I might be willing to grant him that power as long as it was checked, first and foremost through congressional oversight," said Lee Hamilton. "What I would not be willing to do is give the president the authority to make that decision all by himself. That's my general view on the entire issue of balancing security and core values: Power must be checked."

The United States is not the first democracy, of course, to find itself compromising core values under an assault by terrorists. European allies have a long history of fighting terrorism, and, in a number of cases, responding with official excesses. The question is what America might learn from their experiences.

"In the mid-1990s, senior officials in the Spanish government engaged in a 'dirty war' of assassination of terrorists belonging to ETA, and no single initiative fighting this terrorist organization was more damaging to the image of the Spanish state or more helpful in generating sympathy and resources for the terrorists," said Fernando Reinares. The painful recovery from that episode took many years and required the conviction and imprisonment of a number of high-ranking Spanish officials and policeman.

"British security services conducted a similar 'dirty war' in Northern Ireland against the IRA, and likewise provoked a backlash of anger that benefited the terrorists," added Reinares. "From that perspective, if you look at public opinion in Europe and the Muslim world concerning the United States's war on terrorism, you see a similar backlash against methods that I believe are counterproductive."

Given France's decades-long experience in combating Islamic extremist terrorism, the Council on Global Terrorism member most sympathetic to the need to forcefully gain the upper hand against terrorists is Xavier Raufer. Yet Raufer also judges that the United States has gone too far.

"If the U.S. had a colonial tradition, then it might have an institutional memory of the brutality and violence that was necessary for France and other powers to keep their colonies," he said. "There are similarities with today's struggle against a global jihadist insurgency. But in the information age, a democracy cannot indefinitely maintain these types of policies without doing lasting damage to itself and its cause. For two or three years it was understandable that the United States would try and extract all of the useful information possible from these prisoners, but the time has come to either prosecute them or send them home. It has simply gone on too long."

More broadly, U.S. officials and the American public may need to adjust their mind-set and move away from the idea that these extraordinary measures put in place in the shadow of 9/11 could somehow crush or eliminate the threat of Islamic extremist terrorism. "This conflict will likely last many, many years, and that means we have to fashion a more sustainable effort that maintains the support of the general public and our vital allies," said Brian Jenkins. "To achieve that we have to stay true to our core values, because if we violate them we risk alienation, isolation, and, ultimately, defeat. Core values should not be viewed as a constraint in this conflict, but rather as a source of our strength. And refusing to barter them for an extra measure of security is not just a matter of morality; it's a strategic imperative." ∎

# Reversing Islamic Radicalization 7

| | |
|---|---|
| OVERALL GRADE | **D–** |

| | |
|---|---|
| Preventing the export and spread of intolerant Wahhabism | D |
| Countering the impact of radical Imams, mosques, and madrassas | D |
| Combating the spread of radicalism in prisons | D– |
| Destroying bin Laden's image as an Islamic hero | D |
| Managing the Sunni/Shiite divide within Islam to counter the sway of extremists in both camps | F |
| Supporting moderate and reformist Muslims to help them counter radical ideologues in the struggle for Islam's future | D+ |
| Minimizing the radicalization of second generation immigrants | D– |
| Preventing terrorist use of internet for recruitment and propaganda | D– |

Despite everything accomplished over the past five years in the U.S.-led global "war on terror," the Council believes that we are losing ground in the campaign to contain violent Islamic extremism. The reason for that collective judgment is failure in the essential task of stemming the tide of radicalization in the Islamic world. That tide is fed by strong currents of humiliation, anger, and despair among Muslims, and it both replenishes terrorist ranks directly and serves as a wellspring of sympathy and support in which the terrorists operate freely.

"When people talk about the global war on terrorism they often focus on the most tangible aspects, such as fighting wars, hunting terrorists, gathering intelligence, and protecting our borders," said Lee Hamilton. "At its core, this conflict is fundamentally a war of ideas, however, and I don't think we're winning that war. I find that very frustrating, because American ideas and ideals are powerful and compelling, and they should work to our advantage. Unfortunately, we have not conveyed our ideas or shaped our ideals into policies in ways that have improved our relationship with the world's 1.3 billion Muslims."

Evidence of a growing radicalization in the Islamic world is substantive and quantifiable. Data points include the recent deadly riots by Muslims infuriated over cartoon depictions of the Prophet Mohammad published in a Danish newspaper, and extended rioting and vandalism in France by disaffected Muslim youth. In Europe, intelligence officials report a significant rise in radicalized Muslims joining terrorist networks by the hundreds, and perhaps thousands, in order to wage jihad against the U.S.-led coalition in Iraq. In the most recent Pew global attitudes polls, approximately 15 percent of Muslims surveyed in Britain, France, and Spain believed suicide bombings and other forms of violence were at least sometimes justified in the defense of Islam.

The U.S. State Department also reported a sharp rise in terrorist attacks last year, passing the 10,000 mark for the first time. Those terrorist attacks were responsible for 14,500 fatalities worldwide, with 25,000 additional people wounded and maimed. The unusually high casualty rate was due in part to the ongoing conflict in Iraq, and to a dramatic increase of terrorists willing to "martyr" themselves in suicide attacks. In 2005 there were a record 360 suicide bombings, many in places where such radical tactics had rarely, if ever, been seen before, including Afghanistan and London.

Of equal concern is the growing number of self-starter cells of Islamist terrorists with no connection to al-Qaeda or other formal terrorist groups, other than a shared embrace of a radical ideology and a willingness to kill innocent civilians in pursuit of those beliefs. Such groups of homegrown terrorists played major roles in the murder of Dutch filmmaker Theo van Gogh in November 2004 and the foiled July 2005 bombing plot in London, and recently were the target of police crackdowns in Canada, Australia, and Miami, Florida.

Council member Xavier Raufer noted the exalted status that Osama bin Laden has achieved among the Islamic diaspora of Europe. "In terms of French Muslims, the most radicalizing idea we confront is this mythology that has built up around bin Laden as a sort of Islamic Robin Hood," he said. "At a time of significant agitation and frustration in the Islamic community, bin Laden gives them a sense of empowerment. By urging Muslims everywhere to strike a blow against the West, he offers them a catharsis. This emergence of bin Laden as an iconic Islamic hero is very troubling."

The escape of top al-Qaeda leaders Osama bin Laden and Ayman al-Zawahiri from Afghanistan in 2001, and their success in eluding capture or death ever since, have elevated them as symbolic firebrands for radical Islam. Though U.S. and coalition efforts to target al-Qaeda's leadership and deny it sanctuary in Afghanistan are positives, both top al-Qaeda leaders—through periodic releases of video- or audiotaped statements—remain chief propagandists for the radical cause and catalysts to terrorism.

"The communications from bin Laden and Zawahiri have become both more frequent and more sophisticated, and they are benefiting from this narrative that the top al-Qaeda leaders have survived the infidel's mightiest blows," said Brian Jenkins. In the past year, he noted, bin Laden has released five communications, and al-Zawahiri nine, and their messages are increasingly tailored for specific audiences. "We have to remember that this conflict is essentially a missionary enterprise for bin Laden and Zawahiri, and there is ample evidence that their flock is growing. There's no question that bin Laden's extremist ideology is more discussed today than at the time of the 9/11 attacks."

The backdrop for all that increased radicalization, and the growing pool of sympathizers, is a yawning gap in perception between the West and Muslim worlds. Bin Laden has skillfully exploited that break, and the very different views it represents, to further his fevered dreams of a "clash of civilizations."

"Years ago, when they actually had free elections in Pakistan, the extremists rarely ever garnered more than 5 percent of the vote," said Xavier Raufer. "Contrast that with today: From Pakistan to Algeria, we're seeing radical Salafist ideology steadily making inroads into the general Muslim population. You can see the gains even in the length of men's beards or the way women dress. That doesn't mean all of those people are terrorists, but they embrace the same puritanical brand of Islam. That ideology is the fertile earth in which Islamic terrorism is now growing."

Remarkably, in the same Pew poll mentioned earlier, majorities in countries considered key U.S. allies in the Muslim world (Turkey, Egypt, Jordan, and Indonesia) said that they did not even believe that groups of Arabs carried out the 9/11 terrorist attacks.

## Sources of Radicalization

To understand why more and more Muslims are becoming radicalized, one can look to the original currents that fed into the violent Islamic extremism of the 1980s and '90s, culminating on September 11, 2001. Along with a majority of the 9/11 hijackers, Osama bin Laden is a Saudi who embraces the fundamentalist Wahhabi version of Islam, puritanical in its strictures and extremely intolerant of nonbelievers.

The relationship between the Saudi royal family and Wahhabism is complex, and it touches on that nation's long religious traditions, need for domestic stability, status as the protector of Islam's most holy places, and competition with Shiite Iran in the realm of Islamic theology. The results of that complex relationship, however, are unambiguous. For many years, the Sunni rulers of Saudi Arabia allowed the country's vast oil wealth to be used in part to promote and export Wahhabism through the establishment of fundamentalist mosques and religious academies and schools called madrassas.

Nowhere did the export of fundamentalist and intolerant Wahhabi ideology find more welcome than in Pakistan. A poor country with a weak central government unable to provide adequate education to its own youth, Pakistan allowed the Wahhabi-inspired madrassas to fill its educational void. The Pakistani Inter-Services Intelligence (ISI) agency also had a thirty-year history of supporting Islamic militants as a way to wield influence in neighboring Afghanistan and operate in Kashmir (a disputed province where Pakistan and India have fought three wars and countless skirmishes).

After the 1979 Soviet invasion of Afghanistan, the United States colluded with the Saudis and the Pakistanis in helping a worldwide network of radical mosques funnel Islamic militants to Pakistan in order to wage holy war against the Soviet Union in Afghanistan. Following the defeat and eventual withdrawal of Soviet forces, Pakistan's ISI threw its support behind the fundamentalist Taliban as a way to stabilize a fractious Afghanistan.

From this combustible witches' brew of extremist Islamic ideology and violent conflict emerged Osama bin Laden and the Afghan mujihadeen that formed the core of al-Qaeda. Bin Laden recognized that the same worldwide network that funneled Islamic militants into Afghanistan to defeat the Soviet Union could be reversed to wage global jihad against Saudi Arabia. When bin Laden failed to gain any real traction in his battle against the Saudi royal family, al-Zawahiri likewise found little purchase in his attempts to overthrow the Mubarak regime in Egypt, and al-Qaeda made few advances in Yemen, the campaign against the "near enemy" needed to be rethought. With a collapse of the movement imminent, bin Laden and al-Zawahiri stepped back and strategized anew. This led to a shift in focus to the "far enemy," and the United States as a particular target. This new mission got results. All the while, the ebbs and flows in purpose and rhetoric were held together by a puritanical, uncompromising worldview.

## Unresolved Causes of Extremism

That history remains relevant today. For all its accomplishments, the U.S.-led counterterrorism campaign has failed to adequately combat the underlying causes of Islamic extremism manifested in the 9/11 attacks. While Saudi Arabian security forces have energetically joined the fight against al-Qaeda after a series of terrorist attacks on the kingdom in 2003, there is insufficient evidence that the Saudi government has staunched the spread of virulent Wahhabi ideology.

Just this year, Freedom House's Center for Religious Freedom examined Saudi Ministry of Education textbooks used in schools and madrassas within the kingdom and around the world, including Saudi-run academies in nineteen world capitals. Despite proclamations to the contrary by Saudi officials, the report, titled "Saudi Arabia's Curriculum of Intolerance," found that Saudi textbooks continue to promote an ideology of hatred toward anyone, Muslim or non-Muslim, who does not subscribe to the Wahhabi sect of Islam.

Specifically, Freedom House found that the official Saudi textbooks: command Muslims to "hate" Christians and Jews, as well as non-Wahhabi Muslims; teach that "Jews and Christians are enemies of the [Muslim] believers" and that the clash between the two realms is perpetual; and assert that the spread of Islam through jihad is a religious duty.

Likewise, while Pakistani President Pervez Musharraf has become a critical and trusted counterterrorism ally, and has survived two al-Qaeda-directed assassination attempts, the Council on Global Terrorism sees little evidence that the Pakistani government has successfully implemented promised educational and religious reforms in the country's many madrassas.

"I was recently in Pakistan, where nearly half of the children are out of school and a significant number of those children who are in school still attend jihadist madrassas," said Fernando Reinares. "In Saudi Arabia, the political elite have certainly been made aware of the problem of extremist ideology, but their textbooks continue to glorify death and martyrdom."

Those original sources of the current wave of Islamic radicalization, he points out, continue to spread to other nations and regions. "I was also recently in Mauritania and Mali in Africa, a region of the world where Salafist or Wahhabi ideology was largely alien just a few years ago," said Reinares. "Today those countries are seeing a large number of madrassas spring up that are outside the government's control and funded by Saudi and Pakistani capital. So while we continue to focus on police and intelligence work to target today's terrorists, the next generation is already being indoctrinated."

This indoctrination comes not only from the madrassa system that functions with such vibrancy throughout much of the Middle East, South Asia, and Southeast Asia, but also through radical imams both in these regions and in the West. While most continue to preach from the pulpits of established mosques, many of these radicalizing imams create jerry-rigged prayer meetings to indoctrinate new recruits. This leaves them both unaccountable and better able to avoid capture.

In the case of two homegrown terrorist cells that were recently exposed in Australia, for instance, the common thread between them was a radical preacher who exerted influence over both groups and inspired them to radicalize quite quickly. Because such radical imams know that authorities are likely to monitor large mosques, they are increasingly operating out of prayer halls, social clubs, and private homes.

Though there is evidence of significant success in identifying and tracking the actions of some radical imams, many who served as primary facilitators in recruiting and indoctrinating Islamists to al-Qaeda and the jihadist cause in the 1980s and '90s, the problem of itinerant radical preachers persists. Partly this is a reflection of the understandable sensitivity in Western nations toward religious freedom. Yet it also speaks to the difficulty of monitoring radical behavior in a religion that has no formal clergy. In many, if not most, cases of homegrown terrorist cells, however, intelligence and law-enforcement experts say the presence of a radical imam was still the common trigger to radicalization and action. As the sermons are being moved from traditional venues into the kitchens of the believers, the problem becomes all the more difficult to counter as proselytizers leave conventional mosques to evade authorities.

## New Triggers to Radicalism

A related unintended consequence of the struggle against violent Islamic extremism has been the increased use of prisons by al-Qaeda and other captured Islamists as focal points for recruitment and indoctrination. With their large populations of idle, violence-prone, and impressionable men, prisons have been targeted by al-Qaeda as potential hotbeds of radicalization. Council members note precedents in this trend: the ultraviolent Islamic terrorist organization GIA began in Algerian jails; José Padilla, an American suspected of planning to set off a dirty bomb on U.S. soil and currently facing terrorism charges, grew up in Chicago and was converted to Islam in prison.

"In France, the conversion of thousands of prisoners to radical Islam is in many ways worse than the problem we faced with radical mosques in the 1990s, because Islamic radicals literally have a captive audience of young, dangerous men already predisposed to illegal behavior," said Xavier Raufer. "We're now seeing the Islamic equivalent of prison gangs."

This dangerous mixture, so particular to the prison environment, creates a multipronged problem. Many prisons are heavily populated by inmates with backgrounds in drug smuggling and document forgery, capabilities authorities must worry about terrorists acquiring.

A skilled document forger who was radicalized could open the doors for the freer movement of terrorists. The cycle of common criminals turning into radicals while imprisoned is spotlighted by recent research undertaken by Fernando Reinares, who showed that of around 200 people arrested on terrorism-related charges in Spain since 9/11, at least 20 percent were previously imprisoned for entirely unrelated offenses. The conversion of prisoners to radical Islam also threatens to hasten and facilitate potential marriages of convenience between criminal networks and terrorist organizations. In the case of the Madrid bombings of 2004, for instance, the Islamic terrorist cell acquired the actual plastic explosives from the brother of a small-time Spanish crook that one of the cell members met while incarcerated. Council members also note the danger posed by a large prison escape by jihadis held in Mauritania, as well as the release of thousands of former Islamic terrorists from Algerian prisons as part of a reconciliation process in that country.

"While the United States has successfully degraded the operational capabilities of 'al-Qaeda Central,' we've failed to recognize 'jihadism' as a cycle that begins with communication and escalates through radicalization, recruitment, training, and then operations unto death," said Brian Jenkins. "Until we break the cycle at radicalization and recruitment, we will not be successful in this conflict. We can turn some of the people we have in custody around so they actively denounce jihadist recruitment in the same way the reformed gang member or ex-convict goes out to schools and neighborhoods to tell others that it's not the way to go. We can legitimately do that in our society—nothing prevents us from being more active in the areas of rehabilitation and reeducation."

A final trigger to radicalization and violence of growing concern is the Islamic jihadi Web site. After al-Qaeda and its affiliated groups lost their sanctuary in Afghanistan, counterterrorism experts began seeing a proliferation of such Web sites on the Internet. From just a handful at the turn of the century, intelligence experts are now tracking more than 5,000 Web sites today, and that number continues to climb. The radical Islamists are now so adept at using the Internet to recruit, indoctrinate, and communicate that intelligence experts talk about the emergence of a terrorist "sanctuary in cyberspace."

"The United States has focused its public diplomacy outreach on Arabic-language television and radio stations, which are important in terms of keeping Muslim moderates who get their news from traditional sources from becoming radicals," said Bruce Hoffman. "But increasingly the Internet is connecting young Islamists with violent inclinations to one another and giving them a sense of empowerment. Countering these jihadist Web sites in a way that keeps these Islamic radicals from actually reaching the tipping point to violence is critical. The truth is, if we don't reverse the tide of Islamic radicalization we won't have enough bullets to kill all the potential terrorists who might take up arms against us." ▪

# High-Risk Areas 8

OVERALL GRADE **D**

| | |
|---|---|
| Reforming autocratic regimes of the Middle East | **D** |
| Promoting the rise of elected, non-violent political parties | **D** |
| Preventing takeovers of countries by violent extremists | **D** |
| Stemming high-risk areas from becoming hot beds of al-Qaeda-motivated terrorism | **D+** |
| Denying sanctuary and safe havens | **D+** |

The current global jihad by Islamic extremists began with an idea, but needed fertile ground in which to take root and fully flower into the lethal form of terrorism we confront today. The ideological underpinning was borne of Salafi Wahhabism preached in Mecca and exported with Saudi oil wealth to madrassas in the Middle East, South Asia, and eventually around the world. Fundamentalist in its arrested worldview, this offshoot of Sunni Islam is notably racist toward Jews, intolerant not only of "infidels" but also of other Islamic sects, and violent in its call to a distorted version of jihad against nonbelievers.

The ideology of Salafi extremism found its proving ground in Afghanistan. In the 1980s, thousands of eager mujihadeen were funneled from secure areas in Pakistan into Afghanistan to fight the Soviet army. After the Soviets were successfully driven out, the Wahhabi doctrine found its purest expression in governance through the fundamentalist Taliban that came to rule the country. Osama bin Laden eventually turned Afghanistan into an al-Qaeda sanctuary, from which he methodically expanded and exported the terrorist jihad—eventually all the way to America's shores.

In the previous chapter, the Council on Global Terrorism traced the increasing radicalization in the Muslim world, from east to west—the wellspring of the Islamic extremist threat. In this section, we address the high-risk areas where that ideology of intolerance and jihad has most deeply taken root, or is in danger of doing so. We judge efforts to deny sanctuary and dismantle incubators of Islamic extremist terrorism as insufficient in part because al-Qaeda's original beachheads in Afghanistan and Pakistan remain contested. Knowing that "al-Qaeda Central" has always depended on safe havens, whether in its repeated use of Pakistan and the border regions of Afghanistan or its inhabitation of Sudan in the mid-1990s, the ability to deprive Osama bin Laden and his minions sanctuary remains a major failure.

## Afghanistan and Al-Qaeda Unsettled

"The United States and NATO were perfectly justified and right to intervene in Afghanistan, where al-Qaeda enjoyed open-air sanctuary to run training camps and plot attacks for years. But we made a major mistake in not finishing the job," said Fernando Reinares. "Now, five years later, the Taliban is resurgent in areas of southern Afghanistan, and al-Qaeda has increased its attacks in the region. And because we did not do enough to support the Afghan government or improve the living conditions of the people, there are signs that the Taliban are once again gaining sympathy in parts of the country."

Indeed, with the arrival of warmer weather earlier this year, Taliban forces launched their most aggressive offensive in southern Afghanistan since the United States intervened in 2001. The number of U.S. troops who have died in Afghanistan over the past year is more than double the number in 2003 or 2004, and Taliban insurgents have mounted multiple coordinated assaults on U.S. and NATO bases in the country. The arrival of large numbers of Taliban—reportedly flush with money and new weapons—in some southern villages in Afghanistan has also dealt a blow to public confidence in the nascent Afghan democracy. Afghan President Hamid Karzai, a key U.S. ally, has seen his popularity plummet in the last year and announced he will not run for president again in elections slated for 2009.

"Rousting the Taliban from Kabul and denying al-Qaeda what had been a comfortable safe haven in Afghanistan was a good and important achievement, and since bin Laden and his lieutenants are on the run, they are not nearly as well positioned to plan and organize attacks like 9/11," said Paul Pillar. "We can't afford to make the same mistake in Afghanistan today that we made in the early 1990s, however, after the Soviets had left and the United States essentially washed its hands of the country. That allowed the Taliban to rise to power and al-Qaeda to find refuge. So we have to stay engaged and build on the progress we've made. We cannot simply walk away."

Tellingly, a traffic accident in Kabul involving a U.S. military convoy in May sparked riots that left eleven people dead, amounting to the worst demonstrations in the capital since the overthrow of the Taliban. This suggests that the Afghan people are becoming increasingly frustrated by the lack of improvement in their daily lives despite the presence in their country of so many foreign troops. Such frustrations and anger make the Afghan population more susceptible to radical Islamic ideology.

## Pakistan on the Edge

If possible, the situation in neighboring Pakistan is of even greater concern. As the recently foiled jetliner plot revealed, the threads of many major terrorist plans continue to lead back to Pakistan and al-Qaeda. These same ties, even if tenuous, were apparent in the devastating terrorist bombings of the London and Madrid transit systems.

Both Osama bin Laden and Ayman al-Zawahiri, along with many top al-Qaeda lieutenants, are thought to be hiding in the lawless Pakistani tribal regions of Waziristan. Pakistani authorities say they have captured more than 600 al-Qaeda suspects since 9/11, including senior operatives such as 9/11 mastermind Khalid Shaikh Mohammed and 9/11 middleman Ramzi Binalshibh (captured in Rawalpindi and Karachi, respectively); former close bin Laden aide Abu Zubaydah (captured in Faisalabad); operations chief Abu Faraj al-Libbi (captured in Mardan); communications engineer Muhammed Naeem Noor Khan (captured in Lahore); strategist and propagandist Mustafa Setmariam Nasar (captured in Quetta); and the planner of the 1998 U.S. embassy bombings in Africa, Ahmed Khaifan Ghailani (captured in Gujrat). Earlier this year, U.S. forces launched missiles into the Pakistani border village of Damadola, reportedly barely missing al-Zawahiri but killing a number of his top aides, including al-Libbi's successor, Hamza al-Rabie.

Despite strenuous efforts, the Pakistani government has been unable, so far, to exert effective control over its western tribal regions, which are now a sanctuary for al-Qaeda and a base of support for bin Laden. After the Pakistani government sent more than 70,000 troops into the frontier region on its western border with Afghanistan in fall 2005, fierce fighting with tribal forces left more than 300 Pakistani soldiers dead. Meanwhile, Musharraf's counterterrorism alliance with the United States remains deeply unpopular with the Pakistani public.

"Pakistan's tribal territories near the border with Afghanistan have essentially been ungoverned since the British Raj more than 150 years ago," said Xavier Raufer. "The United States has discovered that it's an area where you can't invade, yet it is just such ungoverned or 'no go' areas that the terrorists most like to exploit as sanctuary."

Indeed, the rest of Southwest Asia and the Indian subcontinent remain fertile ground for the potential spread of Islamic extremist terrorism. The investigation into the recent terrorist bombings in Mumbai, India, for instance, revealed that Islamic extremist groups in Pakistan have been actively recruiting among the 120 million Muslims in India, many of whom feel persecuted by the Hindu majority there and are upset about India's increasingly close strategic relationship with the United States.

The Mumbai bombings also indicate that Kashmiri jihadis, yet another al-Qaeda affiliate, still have a robust capability. The conflict in Kashmir persists, and while all the details of the Mumbai bombings are yet unclear, it is likely the expression of a common ideology expressed through Lashkar-e-Taiba. This problem is becoming so pernicious that we are seeing it beginning to sprout up in the United States. In northern Virginia, a group associated with LeT was using paintball games to prepare and train for attacks.

Meanwhile, in Asia, there are signs that members of Jemaah Islamiyah have found refuge in the southern Philippines, and concerns continue to mount that jihadis may be drawn to the battle between a resurgent Taliban and coalition forces in Afghanistan. And, of course, counterterrorism experts around the world fear that it will not end there; rather, Iraq could become the next terrorist incubator.

## Terrorist Incubators

If Pakistan continues to top the list of high-risk areas, given that its territory serves as sanctuary for al-Qaeda, Iraq looks disturbingly like the incubator for global jihad that Afghanistan proved to be in the 1980s. Once again, global Islamic extremist networks are funneling terrorists and would-be martyrs to a Muslim country to do battle with forces they view as non-Muslim occupiers. A new generation of jihadis are learning the terrorist craft and networking with one another in a near-perfect environment of extreme violence, mayhem, and weak governmental control. Once again the armed forces of a global superpower are bogged down in a foreign land and engaged in the equivalent of a bloody knife fight with insurgents and terrorists.

"Osama bin Laden has made very clear that he views Iraq as the same graveyard for U.S. forces that Afghanistan proved for the Soviets," said Brian Jenkins. "He knows (guerrilla) forces can't defeat us on the battlefield, but we are engaged in precisely the kind of warfare that insurgents and terrorists wage best, and they hope to make our position in Iraq untenable. Like the Soviets in Afghanistan, they anticipate our withdrawal from Iraq as a step towards our ultimate collapse. In fact, it took the mujihadeen ten years to drive the Soviets out of Afghanistan, and I don't believe bin Laden thinks the United States has that kind of staying power in Iraq."

In the meantime, Jenkins said, those Islamic extremists not killed by U.S. and coalition forces in Iraq are honing their skills with on-the-job training in much the same fashion that made the Afghan veterans so formidable as terrorists. "In any (guerrilla) or terrorist organization, the key driver for learning and acquiring fungible knowledge is how frequently you conduct operations." In Iraq, officials are now seeing an average of about ninety insurgent attacks each day, which, Jenkins said, "represents a lot of opportunities for learning and improvement, and indeed we're already seeing lots of innovation in the way the insurgents and terrorists are bombing and sabotaging infrastructure in Iraq. So in addition to the danger that Iraq will prove the kind of bonding experience that holds these extremists together for many years to come, much like Afghanistan proved for bin Laden's generation of terrorists, we also have to worry that they are perfecting their techniques and will eventually disseminate that knowledge throughout the global jihadist community. That's a very serious concern."

In addition to the tumultuous environments in South Asia and Iraq, the war between Israeli forces and the terrorist group Hezbollah this summer solidifies the Council on Global Terrorism's rating of the Middle East as the most dangerous region in the world in terms of the terrorist threat. The fighting in Lebanon also reveals just how far short of the mark the U.S.-led war has fallen in discouraging state sponsorship of terrorist groups. Hezbollah, formed in 1982 by Iran's Revolutionary Guard to serve as a proxy in fighting Israeli forces in southern Lebanon, rapidly gained strength and expertise backed by massive support from its progenitor and Syria. Collusion between these states and Hezbollah continues today.

Most troubling, U.S. intelligence services have found evidence of some cooperation between Hezbollah and al-Qaeda, even though the two groups stand on opposite sides of Islam's Shiite-Sunni divide. Hezbollah is a multifaceted organization whose shape and agenda have evolved over its decades-long lifespan. Originally concerned with Israel's occupation of Lebanon, it also targeted American soldiers and civilians (the 1983 bombing of Marine barracks in Beirut that killed 241 Marines and the 1996 terrorist bombing of the Khobar Towers in Saudi Arabia being the two most infamous and deadly incidents). Hezbollah now appears to be leading the charge in a resurgent Shia terrorist threat. How different any renewed Shia terrorism by Hezbollah will be from al-Qaeda- and Sunni-inspired terrorism, or what links it might have to the latter, is still unclear.

"I think it's nothing more than wishful thinking to say that Hezbollah has moderated," said Bruce Hoffman. "The crisis in Lebanon and Gaza is tailor-made to suit their agenda. Just when it looked like we were making some progress in stabilizing Lebanon's democracy, Hezbollah has once again provoked a crisis and an Israeli response that has driven a wedge between the U.S. and many of its allies and partners, and has diverted attention from Iran's nuclear program. And given the radical views expressed by Iranian President Mahmoud Ahmadinejad, we have to assume there's a strong signal coming from Tehran for Hezbollah to pursue a more radical agenda in Lebanon and elsewhere in the region as well."

## Ungoverned Spaces

Counterterrorism experts worried about a future replication of the "Afghan model"—a weak central government, conflict between Muslim and non-Muslim populations and forces, terrorist activity, and large ungoverned spaces—must also look at Africa with concern. In fact, the Afghan model is an apt description of virtually the entire area stretching from Mauritania and Mali in the west, through Niger, Chad, and Sudan, and all the way to the Horn of Africa in the east—a restive region larger than the entire United States.

Numerous trends within that area point to trouble. In Somalia, which has not had a viable central government in more than a decade, a network of Islamic tribunals, the Islamic Courts Union (ICU), recently consolidated its hold on Mogadishu and much of the rest of the country after defeating U.S.-backed warlords. In addition, there are reports that the ICU is instituting Islamic sharia law and may be moving toward the installment of a Taliban-type government. Deepening concern, the ICU reportedly holds within its ranks al-Qaeda operatives with ties to the 1998 terrorist bombings of U.S. embassies in Tanzania and Kenya.

Much of the rest of the region is no better off. In Sudan, Islamic militias backed by the Arab government in Khartoum are accused of committing genocide in their attacks on non-Muslim Africans in the south of the country and to the west in Darfur. In the western trans-Sahara, remnants of Algeria's brutal Islamic terrorist group (the

GIA) and its offshoots roam throughout the vast ungoverned spaces of northern Mali and Niger.

"Any area that appears to replicate the Afghan model has to be considered a major concern, because it could become a sanctuary for al-Qaeda and associated terrorist groups to set up training camps and operations," said Walter Reich. "Certainly Somalia and parts of the trans-Sahara fit that description of a sort of no man's land."

In an age of global terrorism, these shadowy areas where no governments hold sway and the civilized world would rather avert its gaze, ignorance comes only at great peril. "If you look at the sources of the threat we face from nonstate actors it comes most directly from these uncontrolled areas of the world," said Xavier Raufer. "It might be the tribal territories on the border between Pakistan and Afghanistan; or the Golden Triangle between Thailand, Laos, and China; or states that are not real states, such as Bosnia-Herzegovina. And the threat they represent comes not only from terrorism; it's also from drug smuggling, human trafficking, illegal arms trading, and organized crime. This growing threat emanating from the world's ungoverned spaces has not been taken seriously enough." ∎

# Shaping Long-Term Solutions

9

| | OVERALL GRADE | D |
|---|---|---|
| Addressing long-term causes of Islamic radicalization, be they economic, religious, political, or societal | | D |
| Helping Muslims in the West assimilate | | C |
| Implementing foreign policy necessities while minimizing anger in the Muslim world | | F |
| Countering conspiracy theories and anti-Americanism with overt and/or covert public diplomacy | | D– |
| Decreasing U.S. dependence on oil | | F |

To concede that there are underlying conditions that help give rise to Islamic extremism in no way justifies the use of terrorism or absolves terrorists from responsibility for their heinous acts. It does not shift the blame for the murder of civilians from the terrorists to their accused oppressors, nor does it suggest that social conditions such as poverty, political disenfranchisement, or territorial disputes lead inexorably to terrorism. The evidence is clear that in most instances they do not. Yet many members of the Council on Global Terrorism believe that a counterterrorism strategy that ignores the conditions that help spawn Islamic extremism and are exploited by the terrorist propagandists is unlikely to succeed in the long term.

In many ways, combating the so-called root causes of Islamic extremist terrorism is the most ambiguous and challenging front in this conflict. Even within the ranks of the terrorists, different people turn to violent extremism for different and often deeply personal reasons. One person's standard grievance can be another's tipping point to terrorism. The social, political, and religious roots of Islamic extremism also run deep, are intertwined, and remain impervious to quick fixes or easy solutions. For these reasons, efforts on this front may not bear productive fruit for many years to come, and then often in indirect and hard to quantify ways, causing at least some Council members to question what priority addressing root causes should occupy in the United States's counterterrorism strategy.

"I think it's perfectly natural to want to understand your enemy's motivations, or what some people call the root causes of Islamic terrorism, but I think it would be a grave mistake to assume we can simply modify those motivations in a way that causes the terrorist attacks to stop," said Walter Reich. A corollary impulse is the questionable assumption that if the United States and its allies simply satisfy certain demands or goals of the terrorists, their activities will cease. "I don't think we can allay the motivations or satisfy the goals of Islamic terrorists, partly because satisfying those goals only elicits additional demands in an endless cycle, and partly because the main reason terrorism is practiced is because it actually works. It's cheap and effective. I believe the only way we will ultimately bring it under control is to change the dynamic so that terrorism doesn't work so well anymore."

Even given those qualifications, however, a more common view among members of the Council on Global Terrorism is that if the United States does not try to better understand and address the interplay of conditions that give rise to Islamic extremist terrorism, it risks winning the tactical battles and losing the strategic "war of ideas" that is central to this conflict.

"I believe that terrorists basically act out of grievances, either legitimate or illegitimate," said Lee Hamilton. "Right now I don't see the United States and its allies removing those grievances, and in some cases we've created new ones. If that situation continues, I think the terrorism we are confronting will last a very long time and become a generational problem with which my children—and I daresay my grandchildren—will probably have to cope."

## Ending Tyranny

The Bush administration has made the end of tyranny and the spread of freedom and democracy its signature long-term solution for the problem of Islamic extremism, and its lodestar in waging the global "war on terror." There is compelling reasoning behind an approach that plays to American ideals and traditions of democratic pluralism. Inarguably, much of the Islamic extremist terrorism and its attendant ideology that has bedeviled us for the past thirty years originated from countries in the Middle East and South Asia whose authoritarian governments brook little dissent and offer negligible space for opposing political voices or movements. Many of these governments have maintained domestic stability by venting the subsequent frustration and anger of their citizens outward at the United States and its allies—with Israel a frequent target.

"The terrorism we are confronting is centered in autocratic regimes in the Middle East and South Asia, which have closed systems that frustrate people's aspirations politically, economically, and socially. Young people especially, who might otherwise find peaceful ways to express themselves, thus gravitate to extremist groups as the only way to have a voice and an impact," said Paul Pillar. "I view it as positive that the Bush administration and U.S. policy elites have come to recognize that the old bargain of supporting autocratic regimes in the Middle East, largely in exchange for ready access to oil, was really not much of a bargain after all. A lesson of 9/11 was that it's not just about the oil. We also have to worry about the political configuration in these countries."

Five years into this conflict, one can look back and see both successes as well as setbacks in the Bush administration's campaign to promote the spread of democracy. On the positive side, there have been free elections in Afghanistan, Iraq, and the Palestinian territories. For the first time, women were also recently allowed to vote in Kuwait, and there have been liberalizing reforms in Jordan. Libya has renounced its past support for terrorism, along with its programs for WMD. A popular uprising led to the expulsion of Syrian troops in Lebanon and the diminishment of Syrian influence on that country's fledgling democracy. Unfortunately, much of that progress is now in jeopardy in the aftermath of clashes between Israeli and Hezbollah forces. This reflects much of the to and fro of progress and regression common in these political systems.

On this negative side of the roster, there has been significant backsliding from democratic reforms in Egypt, a marginalization of democratic reformers in Iran, and little movement on full-blown reforms in Saudi Arabia. In addition, elections in Iraq, Egypt, Jordan, and Lebanon have strengthened the hand of fundamentalist Islamic parties. The Palestinians elected the Islamic militants of Hamas to head their government, and the Muslim Brotherhood did particularly well in parliamentary elections in Egypt at the end of last year.

The recent crisis in Lebanon also indicates how readily Islamic extremist groups such as Hezbollah can hijack a nascent democratic process. Having won fourteen seats in parliament during the most recent elections, and holding two ministerial positions in the cabinet, Hezbollah has gone on to behave as an autonomous militia unimpeded by government strictures. Especially in Afghanistan and Iraq, the United States and its allies have also discovered firsthand the monumental difficulties of planting the flag of democracy in countries that have no democratic institutions or traditions, and few of the practices of modern civil societies.

"What we've discovered is that democratic elections absent democratic institutions and habits don't necessarily produce moderation, and in fact can have the opposite effect," said Bruce Hoffman. "As a result of elections, we've seen extreme fundamentalist Islamic groups gain strength in Egypt and Jordan, and a terrorist group elected to office in the Palestinian territories. Looking back, I think the ease of initial military operations in Afghanistan blinded us to the complexities and difficulties of the nation building that would be required to construct viable democracies. In that sense, this conflict is indeed beginning to look less like World War II and more like the Cold War, which was a half-century struggle with a large ideological component."

The past five years have also shown just how perilous a diplomatic tightrope the United States walks in promoting democracy in the region, even while it continues to support a number of autocratic regimes in exchange for ready access to oil or other foreign-policy considerations.

"The United States will always be seen in the region as somewhat hypocritical on the subject of democracy, because a very large gap between our rhetoric on democracy and our policies is built into the equation," said Lee Hamilton. "If you look at Saudi Arabia, for instance, we simply must have access to the oil that country produces at an affordable price, which is why every American president has supported the Saudi royal family and accepted that Saudi Arabia is critical to our national interests. That's a fact of life."

Nevertheless, Hamilton believes, the United States must strive much harder to support those elements in Muslim societies that are moving toward liberalizing change, and continue to pressure their governments toward more openness and transparency. "The United States needs to be on the side of pragmatic reforms in these countries, recognizing that each will present a different set of challenges and that there are limitations to how far we will go in altering U.S. policy. But right now we have neither our public diplomacy nor our foreign policy right in terms of conveying to the average Muslim or Arab that we want a better life for them."

Of course, U.S. support for democracy in the Middle East would seem far more credible and less hypocritical if it were not tempered by the need to so strongly support autocratic regimes in oil-producing nations. A serious effort to reduce America's dependence on oil from the region would thus help greatly in shaping long-term solutions to the problem of Islamic extremism.

"Our oil dependence helped shape the political and economic structure of the Middle East today, which bears directly on the creation of the Islamic extremist terrorism that we are confronting," said Paul Pillar. "Until we reduce our dependence on oil from the region, we will thus always be in a position of weakness in pushing for reform in the Middle East."

## War of Ideas

The Council on Global Terrorism believes that winning the war of ideas is a critical component in defeating Islamic extremism and its underlying ideology in the long term. The United States and its allies must find more effective ways to counteract Osama bin Laden's message by conveying that Western values are not at odds with Islam. Indeed, the United States and its allies have frequently come to the aid of Muslims in places like Afghanistan, Kuwait, and Bosnia. We also need to do more to delegitimize terrorism (especially in the eyes of the Muslim world), drawing attention to the fact that most victims of Islamic extremist terrorism are increasingly fellow Muslims.

"One of the major developments in global terrorism of the past few years has been that attacks by jihadi terrorist groups related to al-Qaeda are killing far more Muslims than non-Muslims, and there has been polling data in Jordan, Iraq, and elsewhere that showed they were losing sympathy among Muslims as a result," said Fernando

Reinares. "In addressing Muslim communities, we in the West have not stressed nearly enough that the brutality of the Islamic terrorists is visited most upon Muslim populations."

The U.S. government has taken some steps to bolster its public diplomacy and named President Bush's close confidant Karen Hughes to the position of undersecretary of state for public diplomacy and public affairs. Congress has also expanded Arabic-language content and outreach to the Islamic world through Voice of America and Radio Free Europe/Radio Liberty stations. Yet, despite these and other efforts, there is strong evidence that we are losing the war of ideas so central to this conflict. We are still too slow and ineffective at countering the lies and conspiracy theories skillfully propagated by bin Laden and other extremist ideologues. As a Pew Center poll reveals, practically the only thing Muslims and Westerners agree on at this point in history is that relations between them are bad, and have gotten worse in recent years.

America's position as the world's lone superpower with interests around the globe and a culture that is broadcast across the world's television and movie screens is guaranteed to cause resentments and tensions even in the most benign of times. There is little doubt, however, that opposition to U.S. foreign policies is also behind the steep rise in anti-Americanism, especially among Muslims. That tide of anti-Americanism threatens to drown out our positive ideas and messages.

In a period of global conflict, with the United States leading a counterterrorism coalition and engaged militarily in two Muslim nations, that spike in resentment was perhaps predictable. That is not necessarily to suggest that it was wrong to intervene in Afghanistan, or for that matter to invade Iraq. Rather, it is to recognize that a superpower's foreign policies have wide-ranging implications and unintended consequences that need to be better understood and mitigated. Unintentional or not, the anger provoked by U.S. foreign policies increases the pool of potential terrorist recruits.

Better understanding the trade-offs between aggressive action and its attendant ramifications will be essential to finding the balance between hard and soft power that is necessary to defeat any insurgency. "We had better start conceding that this struggle looks a lot more like a global counterinsurgency than a war on terrorism, and that means our strategy must be driven more by the ideological dynamic and the battle for hearts and minds in the Muslim world than by direct military action to try and decapitate and attrite very adaptive terrorist organizations," said Bruce Hoffman.

## Iraq: Lightning Rod

In the realm of unintended consequences and collateral damage to the United States's image in the world, the Iraq War stands out. Both the U.S. government and al-Qaeda's leadership have pledged to make Iraq the central battlefield in this conflict, and that is well on its way to becoming a reality. On the front lines, the U.S.-led coalition has recorded significant victories, including toppling a tyrant with a history of terrorist acts who coveted and used WMD. Many foreign jihadis have also been killed in Iraq, most notably the arch terrorist and leader of al-Qaeda in Iraq, Abu Musab al-Zarqawi. Yet we know that the war creates new terrorists every day while Iraq slips deeper into anarchy.

On the ideological front and in the realm of Islamic radicalization, it must be noted that the Iraq War has caused severe damage to the United States's standing in the world, with tangible effects on the ability of Washington to effectively lead in the struggle against violent Islamic extremism. Nightly images of extreme bloodshed and battles between U.S. forces and the Iraqi insurgency, broadcast throughout the Islamic world by Al Jazeera and other unsympathetic Arab networks, have fed into Osama bin Laden's narrative of a modern-day "crusade" waged by the West. Attendant controversies such as the Abu Ghraib prison scandal and the alleged murder of innocent civilians by U.S. Marines in Haditha have further tarnished America's image in the eyes of the world, but especially among Muslims.

If Iraq eventually evolves into a stable democracy with a liberalizing influence on the authoritarian regimes of the Middle East, it could still prove a critical part of the long-term solution to violent Islamic extremism. Conversely, if U.S. forces withdraw from Iraq prematurely before the Iraqi government and security forces are able to fill the vacuum in power, Iraq could turn into the kind of terrorist sanctuary and incubator that Afghanistan proved to be in the 1980s and '90s; indeed, it may well be happening already. In the meantime, it cannot be denied that Iraq has become a lightning rod for the radicalization and recruitment of Islamic militants.

"In the category of policies the U.S. can most directly affect in order to improve the long-term outlook on radicalization and terrorism, Iraq is clearly in a class by itself. There's no getting around that fact," said Paul Pillar. Finding positive and fair resolutions to conflicts in Iraq and between Israelis and Palestinians, he said, "would address the two most salient issues that color perceptions of the United States in an unfavorable way that feeds into extremist Islamic ideologies. The challenge is we have other considerations than just counterterrorism that must be taken into account when fashioning balanced policies on Iraq, the Israeli-Palestinian conflict, and other issues. That's why it's so important to understand all the trade-offs involved."

Brian Jenkins said that pointing out the trade-offs and the counterterrorism costs of a given policy is quite different from arguing for a wholesale policy reversal: "In my view, the remedy of an ill-considered invasion of Iraq is not an ill-considered withdrawal that leaves behind chaos. Likewise, just because bin Laden has often used our close relationship with Saudi Arabia or support for Israel in his propaganda doesn't mean we should change those policies. The United States decides what is in its own national interest, not some terrorist hiding in Waziristan. We should recognize, however, that we do pay a price for those choices."

One way to mitigate those costs might be to renew efforts at reconstruction that tangibly improve the lives of ordinary Iraqis while searching for symbolic gestures and messages of outreach. Nowhere is the brutality of the Islamic extremists associated with Sunni al-Qaeda more on display than in the wanton slaughter of

Iraqi Shiites and the destruction of Shia mosques and holy places in the nation.

"The hypocrisy of al-Qaeda and its affiliates in their willingness to slaughter Shiites and other Muslims they deem as apostate is a real vulnerability, because it counters this narrative bin Laden has projected of a war between the West and a united Islam," said Jenkins. The fact that bin Laden released a seventy-page document trying to justify al-Qaeda attacks in Saudi Arabia that killed mostly Muslims, he said, also indicates that they are sensitive to the issue. "Al-Qaeda-affiliated attacks in places like Egypt, Jordan, Morocco, Indonesia, and Iraq have indeed killed far more Muslims than 'infidels,' and that underscores how they are not really fighting on behalf of Islam, but rather for a narrow and cynical ideology of wanton violence."

## Assimilating the Diaspora

As mentioned earlier in this report, the Council on Global Terrorism believes that efforts under way to better assimilate Muslim populations in Europe and elsewhere in the West are also critical to shaping a long-term solution to the problem of Islamic extremist terrorism. Given the different approaches undertaken by many nations in Europe, allies will need to share their experiences and develop "best practices."

In the case of Spain, the government established an Islamic Commission in 1992, which was strengthened following the Madrid train bombings in 2004. That commission, experts say, has improved communication between the Spanish government and its Muslim population.

"The Islamic Commission was designed both as a way for Muslims to better articulate their collective interests and needs and for the government to better understand and regulate Islamic communities," said Fernando Reinares. "The government provides resources and helps build mosques or offers Spanish-language teachers for Muslim children. In turn, Islamic commissioners, acting as the elected representatives of their communities, work with the authorities to increase understanding of the Muslim population and contribute to the deligitimization of the jihadi terrorist cause. Through this process, the government has dramatically increased the number of Muslim communities officially registered and recognized from roughly 60 to nearly 95 percent. It has improved intelligence and police efforts tremendously." Expanding the beachhead of democracy in the Middle East and South Asia; finding fair resolutions to conflicts in Iraq, Afghanistan, and the Palestinian territories; weaning the United States off its addiction to foreign oil; assimilating new generations of Muslim immigrants into liberal Western societies—these efforts will collectively span decades and outlive today's policy makers.

In the meantime, the United States and its allies must continue to take the fight to al-Qaeda and other Islamic extremist terrorist groups in a campaign of unrelenting pressure. If the counterterrorism coalition does not also focus on the strategic horizon with an eye toward shaping long-term solutions and breaking the cycle of radicalization and jihad, however, the Council on Global Terrorism greatly fears that we will condemn future generations to a world of perpetual conflict. ■

# Rating the Future Terrorist Threat

10

OVER THE NEXT FIVE YEARS

Key: 1 = least likely        5 = most likely

| | |
|---|---|
| Rate the probability that the greatest threat of Islamic extremism will emanate from authoritarian societies in the Middle East | 4 |
| Rate the impact of ungoverned territories in weak or failed states on the terrorist threat | 4 |
| Rate the chance of Iraq becoming a terrorist incubator, training ground, and networking haven like Afghanistan | 5 |
| Rate the likelihood that networks recruiting Islamic radicals for war in Iraq and Afghanistan will be reversed to bring seasoned terrorists back to the West | 5 |
| Rate the likelihood that terrorists and criminals will work more closely together | 3 |
| Rate the danger posed by the emergence of new or renewed Shi'a terrorism | 4 |

| | |
|---|---|
| Rate the likelihood that radical Islamic ideology and its sympathizers will continue to spread in the short-term and long-term | 4 |
| Rate the significance of the restive Islamic diaspora in the West to the future terrorist threat | 4 |
| Rate the chance of al-Qaeda launching another successful 9/11-type attack | 3 |
| Rate the chances that terrorists will use WMD against the U.S. or its allies | 3 |
| Rate the chances that terrorists will explode a dirty bomb against the U.S. or its allies | 4 |
| Rate the chances that the increase in suicide bombings will continue and become a mainstay of Islamic terrorist attacks against the U.S. and its allies | 5 |

Where will the terrorists strike next, how will their hatred manifest itself, and what new terrorist foes may we face in the future? Sunni terrorism continues unabated, and the Shiite threat is on the rise. As the years have shown, these terrorists are capable both of reaching back deep into their playbooks to resurrect a past technique or perfect an unsuccessful plot and of thinking up new and novel attack patterns.

"No one knows if we are 'winning or losing' the war on terrorism," said Lee Hamilton. "A few months ago everyone said al-Qaeda was on its last legs, but now it is back again. Who knows what the reality will be a few months from now? This is simply indicative of the conflict and its nature. But that doesn't mean we cannot make some very educated guesses."

The Islamic extremist terrorists' fundamental conception of this war as a centuries-long struggle endows them with unwavering patience—the luxury of time to attack again and again. The imprimatur of past learning is clearly evident. The September 11, 2001, attacks came almost nine years after the 1993 attempt to topple the World Trade Center towers with a massive truck bomb. The idea of flying aircraft into structures already reared its head in a failed 1994 terrorist attack by an Algerian extremist group with close ties to al-Qaeda. In that case, the terrorists hijacked an Air France jet with the intention of flying it into the Eiffel Tower. Yet further examples of this long-term replication and copycatting include the successful bombing of the U.S. Navy warship *USS Cole* by a small watercraft following an almost identical but failed attempt against the *USS Sullivan* earlier that same year. The recently foiled plot to down as many as ten U.S.-bound jetliners from Britain with liquid bombs likewise resurrected an aborted al-Qaeda plot of the 1990s. Indeed, a marked characteristic of the Islamic terrorism we confront today is that its methods and techniques are limited neither by shallow wells of perseverance nor narrow imaginations of its adherents.

"It has been said of novelists that they live lives of imagination and occupy a wonderfully uncharted realm of their own construction, and

I think the terrorists live similar lives of imagination and inhabit their own reality," said Walter Reich. "Experts call this terrorism 'asymmetric warfare,' and that's true in the sense that terrorists are not limited by rules or the strictures of civilization in terms of what they can and cannot do. They have shown themselves willing to use innocent civilians as human shields, to wantonly kill women and children and fellow Muslims, and to launch plots whose goal is the death of hundreds of thousands or even millions of people. There are countless ways the terrorists could attack us next, simply because there are no limits to their imaginings."

With the past as prologue and the future bound only by the creativity and wherewithal of an adaptive opponent, members of the Council on Global Terrorism were asked to rate the likely direction of the terrorist threat over the next five years. What follows are some of the dangers that darken our own dreams.

## Iraq Redux

As mentioned earlier in this report, the threat that Iraq will prove a terrorist incubator and eventually an exporter of global terrorism is deemed extremely high by the Council. Many believe we are already witnessing the first glimmers of this phenomenon. Like Afghanistan in the 1980s, Iraq has become the focal point of the global jihadi movement, which perceives the conflict as a seminal battle between Muslims and non-Muslim occupiers. The steady bloodshed and continuous stream of terrorist attacks in Iraq that routinely include suicide bombings, assassinations, roadside explosions, kidnappings, and sabotage of infrastructure amount to a near-perfect classroom and proving ground for the terrorist arts. And as Osama bin Laden demonstrated with such devastating effect in the 1990s, the same networks that now funnel Islamic extremists to Iraq could easily be inverted, exporting battle-hardened jihadis and terrorists around the world.

"In terms of the global Islamic jihad, Iraq is the big skewing phenomenon right now," said Paul Pillar. "I am very worried that the networks in Europe and elsewhere that we know are funneling Islamic extremists to Iraq in order to fight the U.S. coalition can be reversed. Remember Mohammed Atta [who led the 9/11 attacks] was recruited for training in Afghanistan with the idea that he would eventually join the fight against the Russians in Chechnya. Instead, someone in al-Qaeda saw special promise in him, and Atta was diverted to the attack on the United States. The same thing could be happening today with extremists in the pipeline to Iraq."

"If you read police reports concerning the latest terrorist plots and operations in Europe, what you see are people who were recruited and radicalized on the basis of the Iraq War, and, to a lesser extent, the Afghan war," said Fernando Reinares. "There is no doubt that the number of these radicalized Muslims in Europe who have entered the pipelines for Iraq and Afghanistan has increased. I'm very concerned that they will one day return to Europe and elsewhere having honed the ability to plan and launch major terrorist attacks."

## Suicide Terrorism

The vast increase in suicide terrorism since the 9/11 attacks speaks to the growing threat posed by this tactic, especially among Islamic extremist terrorist groups such as al-Qaeda that embrace it for its lethality, simplicity, and deeply unsettling psychological impact. Al-Qaeda has thus become the first terrorist group in history to successfully conduct suicide attacks on land, at sea, and in the air. As noted by the 9/11 commission, the stunning success of the 9/11 attacks as an instrument of mass murder was completely dependent on the willingness of the nineteen hijackers to martyr themselves.

Certainly that success is not lost on the rest of the terrorist pantheon, especially Islamic extremist groups that have twisted the tenets of Islam to offer heavenly rewards for suicide attackers. As Bruce Hoffman noted in his revised and updated book, *Inside Terrorism*, of all the suicide operations perpetrated between 1968 and 2005, fully 78 percent have been conducted in the years since September 11,

2001. Last year, suicide attacks were launched by thirty-five terrorist organizations, 86 percent of which were Islamic. Whereas twenty years ago suicide terrorism was an extremely rare phenomenon, in 2005 alone there were more than 350 suicide incidents in twenty-four separate countries, from the United Kingdom, Russia, and Italy to Colombia, Singapore, and, of course, Iraq. Worldwide, suicide operations kill about four times as many people as other kinds of terrorism.

"Largely as a result of Islamic extremist groups justifying suicide attacks with theological arguments, we're witnessing this once-isolated tactic becoming the preferred method of terrorism today," said Hoffman. Because suicide attacks are so psychologically disturbing and lethal, as well as inexpensive to mount and easy to execute relative to other attack modes that require a getaway plan, Hoffman believes, their use will continue to increase, especially by Islamic extremist terrorists.

"Before the attacks on the London transit system last year, the British authorities completely dismissed the threat of suicide terrorism, and today I think U.S. authorities are similarly indifferent. But why should Muslims in the United States be immune to the same currents of radicalization that prompted their British counterparts to act? I believe the suicide attackers who struck the World Trade Center and the Pentagon on 9/11 will almost certainly be followed by other suicide terrorists targeting the United States. I view it not so much as an 'if' as a 'when' proposition."

## Dirty Bombs

As previously mentioned, terrorist use of a nuclear weapon represents the ultimate 'low probability, high consequence' scenario when gauging the future threat. Doomsday scenarios involving these weapons, while unlikely, could involve the deaths of tens of thousands, perhaps even millions, of people. For this reason, the threat cannot be overlooked, but easier accessibility to nuclear fissile materials makes a terrorist attack with a dirty bomb highly probable. The Council on Global Terrorism believes this threat is imminent.

Al-Qaeda documents captured in Kabul detailing plans to construct radiological dirty bombs, and foiled al-Qaeda plots in Europe involving toxins such as ricin, cyanide, and botulinum, reveal that the terrorists also continue to search for new and unconventional ways to deal us a crippling blow. Their inherent tendency to try and try until they succeed makes these findings all the more troubling.

Though the explosion of a dirty bomb by terrorists would be much less physically consequential than the detonation of a nuclear bomb, it would still have a devastating impact both through casualties and its impact on the human psyche. While some believe our biggest fear should be the detonation of a nuclear weapon in Washington or Manhattan (and indeed, such an attack would be terribly destructive), the Council believes we cannot focus on this one possibility and assume the rest of the waterfront is covered. A radiological bomb may well be in our future.

## Mideast Cauldron

Recent events in the Middle East underscore why the Council on Global Terrorism believes that for the foreseeable future this region will be a central battlefield, both literally and ideologically, in the conflict with Islamic extremist terrorism. Strong U.S. backing for Israel's actions against Hezbollah in Lebanon has predictably driven a further wedge between the United States and many of its Arab and Muslim allies. In nearby Iraq, U.S. military leaders have expressed concern that the country may be sliding toward civil war. Meanwhile, radicalization continues apace in the region, ever evidenced by the rise, through free elections, of the Islamic extremist group Hamas in the Palestinian territories, the Muslim Brotherhood in Egypt, and Islamist parties in Iraq.

"Whether because of religious, cultural, or nationalistic reasons, this crash course in democracy we've helped push on the Middle

East has led to the election of groups likely to increase instability and work against our interests in terms of counterterrorism," said Walter Reich. "While I still think American diplomats should encourage autocratic regimes in the region to evolve in a more democratic direction, and help these nations build institutions that can support a functioning democracy, it was probably hubris on the part of the American government to think we could suddenly impose democracy on very restive populations that we don't really understand."

The reemergence of the Iranian-backed Shiite terrorist group Hezbollah as a central player in the current Middle East crisis is also of major concern. Such state-sponsored Shiite terrorist groups were predominant in the 1980s, when they shed a lot of American blood and furthered Iran's goal of exporting its revolution. Iran's possible role in agitating Hezbollah in Lebanon, arming Shiite militias in Iraq, and supporting Palestinian terrorist groups also suggests that the Islamist regime in Tehran believes it now has a freer hand to work against American interests, and that it is once again more than willing to exercise it through terrorist proxies.

"We should be careful not to consider bin Laden the only source of terrorism," said Xavier Raufer. "Hezbollah, and Shiite terror groups generally, may be more dangerous than al-Qaeda because they have the diplomatic support of Iran and Syria. Tomorrow or even five years from now, it seems unlikely that al-Qaeda could drop a dirty bomb in New York City, but Hezbollah could do it today."

While an alliance between Sunni and Shiite terrorist groups may seem unlikely in the current political environment, when Sunni terrorists in Iraq are routinely targeting Shiite populations, the eventual convergence of the two camps into a global jihad was a goal Osama bin Laden dreamed about and promoted. "The Sunni-Shiite divide is not as important as many think," said Raufer. "The Hamas and Hezbollah kidnappings were almost certainly coordinated, and the divide between Wahhabis in Saudi Arabia and the Shiites in Persia has been bridged. There has been a bitter dispute between them since the creation of the kingdom of Saudi Arabia, but the same divide does not exist between radicals, who have close ties even at a popular level."

## The Muslim Diaspora

The recent arrest of more than a score of British Muslims of Pakistani ancestry, accused in a plot to blow up transatlantic jetliners, once again highlights the threat of radicalization within the large and, in many cases, restive Muslim diaspora in Europe. Similar homegrown terrorists of North African and Pakistani descent were also involved in the devastating attacks on the Madrid and London transit systems.

The failure to successfully assimilate Muslim populations has become a strategic vulnerability, especially for many states in Europe that have not traditionally thought of themselves as immigrant nations with a strong melting-pot tradition. The children of Muslim immigrants who, as a result, face cultural alienation and economic stagnation pose a ripe recruiting pool for Islamic extremist terrorist groups.

"There is a distinction to be made between first-, second-, and third-generation immigrants," said Fernando Reinares. "Among the first-generation immigrants, we see people who are alienated because they had high economic expectations that are not being met. Without doubt, relative deprivation is one of the sources of discontent that can be politicized and radicalized into jihadist terror. The second and third generations—children of immigrants—find their discontent not so much in relative economic deprivation as much as in cultural alienation."

There are numerous polls indicating that significant proportions of Muslims in Europe now sympathize with Osama bin Laden and his message of Islamic grievance. "When you have young people who can no longer identify with the culture of the countries where their parents were born, yet they feel neither integrated nor accepted by the societies in Europe where they grew up and now live, then those individuals are very susceptible to recruitment by jihadist groups," said Reinares.

## The Long War

The Council on Global Terrorism also believes there is a danger that the American and allied publics have been conditioned to think of the global "war on terror" as a sprint that can be won in the near term, after which the threat of a terrorist attack will fade. By contrast, we believe this struggle could span decades or even generations, and winning it will require perseverance and an acknowledgment that the threat of terrorist attack will persist. The United States and its allies have faced far greater dangers and vanquished more threatening foes by relying on the strength of free societies united in defense of the values they hold dear.

Brian Jenkins concurred: "Somehow the expectation became that with the extraordinary measures put in place post-9/11, we would crush this threat. Now we realize this conflict requires a much more sustained effort over many years, and that has consequences in terms of allocating resources, maintaining public support, and cooperating with allies. I heard a government official say this conflict is like a wrestling match, and he vowed we would take our enemies down one after another. Well, that analogy is flawed because wrestling meets involve highly regulated combat and only last a few hours. The rules to this game are much less clear, there's no referee to blow the whistle, and we will continue to struggle far into the future." ■

# In Sum: State of the Struggle

| | |
|---|---|
| 1. Combating Islamic Extremist Terrorism | D+ |
| Al-Qaeda headquarters | C+ |
| Al-Qaeda affiliated groups | C– |
| Al-Qaeda seeded groups | D+ |
| Al-Qaeda inspired groups | D |
| Sympathizers | D– |

| | |
|---|---|
| 2. Improving U.S. and Coalition Counterterrorism Capabilities | C |
| Reforming intelligence capabilities | C |
| Improving law enforcement capabilities | C– |
| Transforming military capabilities | C |
| Improving money tracking capabilities | C+ |

| | |
|---|---|
| Cooperation & coordination between branches of government | C– |
| Cooperation & coordination between local, state, and federal government | D+ |
| Cooperation & coordination between allies | B– |

### 3. Creating an Effective Coalition to Fight Terrorism    C–

| | |
|---|---|
| Creating effective, regional counterterrorism coalitions | C |
| Enlisting great powers in the counterterrorism effort | C+ |
| Bringing Muslim nations into the war on terror | C– |
| European Union-U.S. cooperation in the war on terror | B– |
| Passage of effective laws to strengthen international counterterrorism standards | C– |
| Efforts to help willing but weak states better police territory and deny terrorist groups safe havens | C– |
| Deterring state sponsorship of terrorism | C– |

### 4. Preventing Terrorist Attack with Nukes, Dirty Bombs, Germs and Chemicals    C

| | |
|---|---|
| Priority given to preventing terrorists from acquiring CBRN | C |
| Effectiveness of international counter-proliferation policies | C |

| | |
|---|---|
| Efforts to secure nuclear weapons materials in Russia | B– |
| Efforts to stop CBRN technology transfers | C+ |
| Ability to locate and dismantle nuclear proliferation networks | C |
| Ability to prevent WMD scientists from cooperating with terrorists | C– |
| Attempts to deter North Korea and Iran from acquiring nuclear weapons | D– |
| Effectiveness of the Nuclear Nonproliferation Regime | D |

| | |
|---|---|
| **5. Protecting the U.S. Homeland** | **C** |
| Effectiveness of the Department of Homeland Security | C– |
| Increasing aviation security | B– |
| Improving cargo screening | C– |
| Protecting U.S. borders | D+ |
| Improving the ability to track potential terrorists/ dangerous cargo traveling by air and sea | C– |
| Protecting critical infrastructure | C– |
| Increasing the security of mass transit | D– |
| Preventing cyber attack | D+ |
| Improving emergency response to terrorist attack | D+ |

## 6. Balancing Security and Core Values — D+

| | |
|---|---|
| Balance between expanded U.S. counterterrorism authority and respect for civil liberties | D |
| Appropriateness of domestic intelligence gathering in the U.S. | D+ |
| Balance between due process and extraordinary threats | D+ |
| Balance between international law and national security concerns | D– |
| Balance between intelligence gathering through coercive interrogation and respecting commitments against torture | D– |
| Balance struck on these issues by partners in counterterrorism | D+ |

## 7. Reversing Islamic Radicalization — D–

| | |
|---|---|
| Preventing the export and spread of intolerant Wahhabism | D |
| Countering the impact of radical Imams, mosques, and madrassas | D |
| Combating the spread of radicalism in prisons | D– |
| Destroying bin Laden's image as an Islamic hero | D |
| Managing the Sunni/Shiite divide within Islam to counter the sway of extremists in both camps | F |
| Supporting moderate and reformist Muslims to help them counter radical ideologues in the struggle for Islam's future | D+ |

at the Paris Institute of Criminology, University of Paris II. He teaches at the Academy of the French Military Police and is an associate professor at both the École des Hautes Études Commerciales (School of High Commercial Studies), one of the top four business schools in France, and the Chinese People's Public Security University in Beijing and Shenyang.

**Walter Reich** is the Yitzhak Rabin Memorial Professor of International Affairs, Ethics and Human Behavior and a professor of psychiatry and behavioral sciences at George Washington University. He is also a senior scholar at the Woodrow Wilson International Center for Scholars and former director of the United States Holocaust Memorial Museum. Dr. Reich holds positions as a lecturer in psychiatry at Yale University and a professor of psychiatry at the Uniformed Services University of the Health Sciences. He has been co-chair of the Committee of Concerned Scientists since 1995 and has also served as chair of the Committee on Human Rights for the American Psychiatric Association, of which he is a distinguished life fellow. Dr. Reich is editor of *Origins of Terrorism: Psychologies, Ideologies, Theologies, States of Mind.*

**Fernando Reinares** is a professor of political science and security studies at the Universidad Rey Juan Carlos (Rey Juan Carlos University) and director of the Programme on Global Terrorism at the Real Instituto Elcano de Estudios Internacionales y Estratégicos (Elcano Royal Institute for International and Strategic Studies), both in Madrid. Dr. Reinares is chairman of the European Commission experts group on violent radicalization; a member of the academic committee of the Queen Sofía Center for the Study of Violence; a member of the United Nations roster of experts on terrorism prevention; and a member of the Terrorism Studies Programme Board at the University of St. Andrews. From 2004–06, Dr. Reinares served as senior advisor on antiterrorism policy to Spain's minister of the interior. He is a contributing editor of *Studies in Conflict and Terrorism* and belongs to the editorial board of *Terrorism and Political Violence.*

# Index

113